THE DIET...

WEIGHT LOSS BEFORE, DURING, AND AFTER SEX

BY RICHARD SMITH

WORKMAN PUBLISHING, NEW YORK

Design by Paul Hanson

Workman books are available at special discounts when purchased in bulk for premiums and sales promotions as well as for
fund-raising or educational use. Special editions or book excerpts
can also be created to specification. For details, contact the
Special Sales Director at the address below.

Library of Congress Cataloging-in-Publication
data available on request.
ISBN 0-7611-3589-8

Workman Publishing Company, Inc.
708 Broadway
New York, NY 10003-9555
www.workman.com

Printed in the United States of America

First printing: September 2004
10 9 8 7 6 5 4 3 2 1

CONTENTS

BEFORE SEX

I. IN QUEST OF A PARTNER   2

II. PREPARING FOR SEX   17

III. PREPARING FOR YOUR PARTNER   39

IV. SETTING THE SCENE   51

DURING SEX

VI. FOREPLAY 109

VII. INTERCOURSE AND
THINGS RELATED 131

VIII. ORGASM, AND BEYOND   169

AFTER SEX

IX. AFTERPLAY 186

X. SUPPLEMENTARY PLEASURES AND DELIGHTS   212

APPENDIX

THE DIETING LOVER'S LOVE SIGNS 279

INTRODUCTION

If you like exercise, you will like this book. If you loathe exercise, you will love this book.

—DR. RICHARD, FITNESS GURU

Americans may wonder: Why devote precious time to sex when it's golf we really like? We had no choice. That Americans are getting heavier is a fact. That Americans need to have more sex is also a fact. We felt that a book for those seeking to shed pounds in ways more pleasant and productive than, say, video games or high-impact knitting would be helpful for those who hate exercise yet need to lose their love handles.

But just how much weight do we actually lose before, during, and after sex? Although the diet literature and the Internet abound with charts explaining calories burned for everything from jogging (110 calories per mile) to getting your legs waxed (42 calories), similar information for sex has been largely unavailable except to personal trainers in the Food and Drug Administration's witness protection program. Yet, with few exceptions, sex is considered to be the least boring and most pleasurable exercise, not to mention the cheapest and easiest to do, especially if you're on your honeymoon. Indeed, those who've indulged have nothing but praise for its weight loss *and* cardiovascular benefits, and vigorous endorsements—"Totally awesome" . . . "It beats walking to Uruguay in slingbacks" . . . "Far better than medicinal pot" . . . "It's what we plan to do more of when we retire"—are not uncommon.

Make no mistake. The task of compiling these calorie- and carbohydrate-burning counts for so much sexual activity was daunting. We first sought input from several eminent nutritionists, all noted for their irrepressible libidos, but they were unhelpful, choosing instead to lecture us on the glories of onions. We then asked several renowned diet book authors, but they failed utterly. Selected experts in our Spring Break Sex Quiz were unable even to name which part of the female anatomy is best enhanced by a scrunchie. On the essay portion they literally threw up their hands and wept when asked for a scholarly definition of "wet spot," and not one of them knew that winter squash was an aphrodisiac.

Conscientious dieters, therefore, will be happy to learn that *The Dieter's Guide* reflects the latest in weight loss technology plus an increased appreciation of sexual activity—not just for losing weight but for toning the body (our studies show that women over fifty with jiggle-proof upper arms make love at least twenty times a week!) and keeping the complexion glowing (just 32 minutes of sexual activity before going to bed acts as an effective moisturizer and mini-workout). Furthermore, to ensure accuracy, our couples were studied under actual lovemaking conditions. For warm-weather sex, participants performed on vibrating beach chairs in Malibu, their only UVA protection an application of sunblock (SPF 400) and two destitute surfers waving palm fronds. Cold fusion weight loss was determined by locking our volunteer test couple in an unheated cabin on a lake in Bemidji, Minnesota, in February (they emerged 46 pounds lighter, with 200 pounds of fish). And sex-motion studies were performed by observing couples having sex on a campaign bus. (Full disclosure: In many cases, our participating couples got so aroused that electrodes used to determine calorie and carbohydrate counts either fell off or melted. In such cases, we took the liberty of approximating to the nearest decimal point.)

We suggest using this book as an informal guide rather than a rigid manual, making necessary adjustments before, during, and after sexual activity, according to your own individual size, the length of time you indulge (three hours of begging will obviously burn far more calories than one minute of impotence), and whether you have a partner or not. The ability of sexual activity to induce weight loss is best illustrated through the following at-a-glance chart:

SEXUAL ACTIVITY	BURNS OFF
1 hour of foreplay (with panting)	1 medium wedge of key lime pie
30 minutes of intercourse:	
In the two-career couple position (Man on bottom, woman reaching for her laptop)	2 slices of pizza, with everything
In the lotus position (Man on top, lotus on the bottom)	6 ounces of yogurt

Faking an orgasm:	
For her	2 Hershey's Kisses
If she's alone	11 medium burritos
Telling your partner what gets you excited	5 strawberries
Calming your horrified partner	Big pile of corned beef hash
2 hours of bondage:	
Rope	3 margaritas
Floss	2 ounces Diet Pepsi
Philosophy lecture	1 chocolate brownie
Orgasm:	
Regular	1 scone
While selecting new wallpaper	3 scoops of ice cream
Quick fondle	6 peanuts
Hearing little feet running down the hall and a voice asking, "Hi, Mom, whatcha doin'?"	Entire meat loaf plus 2 pounds of kasha varnishkas

Note: Those who believe in neither premarital nor postmarital sex are not good candidates for our weight loss program.

TERMS USED THROUGHOUT

1. "Let the machine get it." Uttered during lovemaking to indicate that things are going too well to take calls from (a) a devoted fan or (b) your ex dialing from the ledge.

2. "Oh, baby, a little to the left" has its ordinary meaning.

3. "Left full rudder" is the nautical counterpart of number 2 above.

4. Mental defect. An affliction that renders the male partner incapable of realizing that the bra he's been trying to remove for the last five minutes unhooks in the front.

5. "Oh, lord, don't stop now." Typical response to a lover who, as his partner approaches climax, asks, "Any meat loaf left?"

6. Deadly physical force. Amount of strength required by a partner wearing sexy attire—black mesh stockings, a see-through camisole, and six-inch spike heels—to drag a reluctant spouse into the bedroom during the playoffs.

7. Double jeopardy. Trying again too soon by an overconfident male, thereby doubling his risk of stroke.

8. Climax. An orgasm without the frills.

9. Chivalry. (1) An act of self-sacrifice in which the male partner, after sex, rolls the female partner over so she can go to sleep. (2) An act of generosity by a male partner who says, "You sleep, honey," and leaves a warm bed at 3:47 A.M. to comfort either a wailing infant or a depressed Peeping Tom.

10. Massage oil. Any FDA-approved substance enabling one to pat, knead, rub, caress, or slide over a partner with fabulous skin tone. Such substances may include but are not limited to aromatic oils, whipped cream, honey, and ski wax.

11. Perjury. Failure to be totally honest when, after sex, a vulnerable male asks, "Was I the best?" (Sadistic women often mention a previous "one-time" lesbian encounter during college.)

12. "So, who does your taxes?" Postlovemaking question least likely to perpetuate the romantic mood. ("Pinochle, anyone?" a close second.)

13. Nooner. Any romantic encounter between noon and 2 P.M. that occurs in a heart-shaped tub or, with workaholics, a heart-shaped cubicle. Also referred to as a working lunch.

14. Fetishism. Sexual excitement produced by fondling a nonliving object such as a shoe or lawyer.

OUR WEIGHT LOSS BONUS SECTIONS

Unlike fad diets, our fitness programs are for all dieters. Those concerned more with carbohydrates and less with calories should pay particular attention to our exclusive Weight Loss Bonus® pages, which list carb grams burned during those lust-intensive activities deemed most efficient for burning off high-carbohydrate edibles like brownies, lasagna, challah, or an exotic woman's earlobe that tastes like marzipan. Some examples:

ACTIVITY	CARB GRAMS BURNED
Example 1:	
Impure thoughts 3	
Acting on them 79	

ACTIVITY	CARB GRAMS BURNED

Example 2:

Putting on a happy face 4

Sitting on a happy face 36

Nutritional Tip: Rare is the lovemaking that cannot be enhanced by the appropriate over-the-counter aphrodisiac, be it protein, carbohydrate, or a judicious combination of both (a breaded Slim Jim, for example). Low-carb dieters who consider themselves merely competent at sex are surprised at the erotic transformation that occurs after just one perfect free-range prune or a tiny bite of squid. Sicilian researchers, on the other hand, report that in the male sex partner, a spicy pesto ravioli favorably affects that portion of the brain known as the "penis."

BEFORE SEX

I. IN QUEST OF A PARTNER

He had plenty of animal magnetism. Unfortunately, it was the kind that attracted badgers.
—WENDY, TAX LAWYER

Finding that one special person for sex (or, if you're indecisive, several special persons) can be difficult. Fortunately, that search for a partner, particularly if you use the Internet (see "Chat Rooms, Leather, and Fruit," Ph.D. thesis by Dr. Hugo Greatfinger, gynecologist-in-waiting, Bryn Mawr), can burn thousands of calories. The horror of a bad blind date (a man who shows up with rice in his hair from his first marriage, for example) can burn up to 700 calories and pare down those love handles that make you think twice about wearing your lucky thong. In the following pages you will see why the search for the perfect lover contributes to weight loss, as well as how, once you meet a partner, even those first intimacies—holding hands, gazing into each other's eyes, meeting each other's friends, fighting for the remote—can continue the weight loss process.

Note: It's a red flag if he calls you for a first date from a pay phone, collect.

SELECTING THE PERFECT DIET PARTNER

Keep in mind that opposites not only attract, but, during sex, consume the most calories. A psychotic flamenco dancer with a tranquil plumber will burn far more calories than a conservative senator with a laid-back pool boy. The table below will help you make the right selection.

YOU	YOUR IDEAL LOVER
Very proper, totally normal, easily freaked by weird behavior; the slightest hint of kinkiness gives you gooseflesh (which burns that hard-to-get-at upper-thigh baby fat).	A man who loves to (a) carry your purse and (b) try on your sun hats. You hate that he looks better than you in your beige-and-white Manolo Blahnik slides.

YOU	YOUR IDEAL LOVER
Drama queen.	Drag queen.
The weak, silent, dysfunctional type, totally passive; can't tell your partner what you really want unless you write it on your Palm Pilot or tentatively point.	Gorgeous, successful, and completely unavailable. A television anchor or an impoverished poet—museum trysts his specialty.
A confirmed prude. You believe sex is for procreation and getting him to paint the kitchen cabinets. During lovemaking you stifle those little stabs of pleasure by biting down on your thumb while reading *Ivanhoe*.	Either a deranged rock star or someone in law enforcement with an affinity for deviant behavior (handcuffs, leather, carrot cake—you know the drill).

YOU	YOUR IDEAL LOVER
A wild, passionate woman. Your maniacal laugh when he or she asks, "What do you really like in bed?" only adds to the merriment.	Finicky. First thing he does after lovemaking is respray his hair. Believes that sex consists of two stages: foreplay and showering.
A philosopher who quilts and listens to Lawrence Welk CDs.	A demon in bed, especially if she's been pregnant for fourteen months.
Vulnerable, innocent waif.	Fading porn star.
Selfish, self-centered, a "But enough about me, let's get back to me" type. Love to lie back and have partner nibble your toes until you achieve critical mass. Afterward you wish him luck as he leaves for obedience training class.	A giver. Takes in stray cats and vagrant mice, gives to the PBA, the UJA, and KGB. Bought 140 cases of Girl Scout cookies. Can't do enough to please his partner, even if it makes him late for the Early Bird Special.

YOU	YOUR IDEAL LOVER
Coy and reserved. You play hard to get by playing hide-and-seek in crowded malls and teeming mosh pits.	Rough, tough, "butch" type with the entire Second Amendment tattooed on her chest.
Untainted. A giving, pink-cheeked Midwest farm-girl type who burns extra calories by carrying around a milk pail.	Beautiful on the outside, not so hot on the inside. A Brooklyn gigolo with great hair and an attitude.
A sixty-three-year-old well-off widow who feels forty years younger.	Twenty-three-year-old aerobics instructor with a tiny IQ and great software.
Insecure.	Never calls.

Note: Be sure your new lover comes with the standard New Lover Warranty: twenty dates or twenty meals, whichever comes first.

BLIND DATES

Certainly one of the more anxiety-inducing events, especially if (a) your friend keeps insisting he has a "great personality" and (b) he shows up with his Yorkie in an infant carrier.

ACTIVITY	CALORIES BURNED
The meeting:	
Just drinks	22
He keeps staring at other women	50
(Burns 25 extra calories if he licks his lips.)	
Dinner:	45
He orders for you	3
Without consulting you	67
He makes an inappropriate sexual advance*:	
Puts his hand on your knee over the table	35
Puts your hand on his thigh under the table	71
Cuts your steak for you	8
Plays his demo tape	60

*Pointing to the "Choking Victim" poster and asking for a naked Heimlich falls under "Inappropriate sexual advance."

Removes food lodged between his teeth:

    With a toothpick 10

    With a plunger 456

Talks only about:

    Sports 14

    Saving the earth 23

    How God loves you 40
    (Subtract 6 calories if you already knew this.)

    His last six relationships
    with those "losers" 66
    (At this point, it's permissible to stuff several
    dinner rolls in your purse and leave.)

WEIGHT LOSS BONUS #1: KNOW YOUR MAN

ACTIVITY	CARB GRAMS BURNED

His credit card is rejected because:

    It's maxed out 10

    It isn't his 58

BREAKING THE ICE

When you finally meet your ideal, you'll know it: *This* is the person I want to be snowed in with. Neglecting your friends and shopping for silly cards are just a few of the well-known symptoms.

ACTIVITY	CALORIES BURNED
Chemistry	100
Long, romantic walks in the rain	49
Sharing an umbrella	20
(Burns 20 extra calories if it's that tiny umbrella from your piña colada.)	
Taking his arm because:	
It feels so nice	8
You're possessive	17
You're blind without your contacts	40
Biceps check	10
Hot e-mails from work	22
Boss lip-reading over your shoulder	248

Holding hands:	8

To remind him he's yours 14

To remind him you still don't
have an engagement ring 130

Carving beloved's initials in tree:	 18

Moving tree-hugger aside 77

Extreme cuddling 25

Weight Loss Tip: Falling in love in the spring burns fewer calories than falling in love in a hardware store.

WEIGHT LOSS BONUS #2: HONESTY EXAM

ACTIVITY	CARB GRAMS BURNED

Biggest lie told by singles:

"I really like my freedom"* 20

*Pertains particularly to:

WOMEN WHO . . .	MEN WHO . . .
Own three or more cats	Own four or more dogs
Save shopping bags	Consider a lava lamp and empty pizza boxes awesome apartment decor

Rely on the kindness of friends to fix them up	Depend on the kindness of friends to trim their hair
Spend New Year's Eve reading *Silas Marner*	Toast New Year's Eve by clinking a beer bottle against a mirror
Are always the first to arrive	Are always the last to leave

THE METROSEXUAL SEX PARTNER

A limited-edition metrosexual (owns patchouli) can easily burn 1,000 calories, especially if, during sex, he constantly glances up at the ceiling mirror to see if he's losing his looks. His efforts to look his best and most seductive for you—the love of his life—are best appreciated by noting the energy he expends on the following activities:

ACTIVITY	CALORIES BURNED
Selecting just the right outfit	48
Hating outfit	60
Choosing new outfit	71
Hoping new Ralph Lauren slacks won't accentuate extra pound gained at health spa graduation	9
Admitting he's powerless over Nilla Wafers	15

ACTIVITY	CALORIES BURNED
Standing in front of full-length mirror	11
Flexing	17
Sucking in	120
Selecting evening's antidepressant:	
Wellbutrin	12
Blond streak	30
Chipping a nail	9
Cursing	66
Application of anti-tug-of-time facial firming cream	14
Wishing it worked	219
Last-minute eyebrow pluck	22
Hoping they don't grow back before sex	98
Final floss	25
Breath check (blowing into empty teacup the preferred method)	3
Spritz of cologne	1
Asking self, "Am I too beautiful?"	6
Yes (*Thank you, Botox*)	13
Attitude check	10
Cleavage check	35

Etiquette Tip: Asking him for decorating advice during sex is inappropriate.

DO ATHLETES DO IT BETTER?

Some typical weight loss figures by profession:

PROFESSION	CALORIES BURNED DURING SEX
Mover and shaker:	
Agent	36
Sandhog	600
Professional athlete:	
Hockey	45
Football	22
Darts	6.1
Socialite:	
New York	162
Washington	50
Tehran	7

PROFESSION	CALORIES BURNED DURING SEX
Mental health professional:	
Psychiatrist	7
Escort	80
Designer:	
Cars	72
Fashion	59
Software	10
Military:	
Pilot	61
Sniper	184
Loose cannon	335
Health care professional:	
Doctor	41
Nurse	90
Mohel	15

II. PREPARING FOR SEX

Sex works on many levels, but for the purpose of our fitness program, we will define sex as any act of intimacy that (a) generates moisture or (b) gets you a fiancé. People, in fact, enjoy sex not just to lose weight but for more practical reasons ranging from surviving Hanukkah to improving their chance of tenure. In this section we provide serious dieters with answers to the hundreds of questions most often asked about sex, including that favorite of curious baby boomers: "I'm over fifty. Do they have large-print sex manuals?"

THE FIVE TOP REASONS FOR SEX

(All Calorie Counts Negotiable)

ACTIVITY	CALORIES BURNED PER HOUR

Desire 412
The most popular form of sex, one that
theoretically should end with a whimper
and begin with a bang. Symptoms include
a zooming heart rate, prolonged moaning,
and a sudden lack of interest in patterns
of federal spending. At its most extreme,
both partners may engage in sexual activities
not yet sanctioned by the Attorney General
or Disney.

Remedial sex 250
Principal motivation here is weight loss,
general shape-up—toning, firming, and
achieving a to-die-for butt—and, if she's
giving you another chance, ego restoration.
Because of its calming effect, remedial sex
makes an ideal relaxant before engaging in
extreme sports such as bungee jumping and
Wal-Mart sale shopping.

Humanitarian sex (aka mercy sex) 124
In this case, sex is administered out of
generosity and with utter disregard for one's
own pleasure. A spouse has just spent twenty-
two hours as a hostage, yet her husband still
has that "Do you want to get frisky?" gleam
in his eye, or an officer has only ten minutes'
leave before returning to his desk at the
Pentagon. After mercy sex, the unselfish
humanitarian often throws in a free Yanni CD.

Obligation sex 99
Sex used in lieu of cash—to pay one's share
of dinner, to make a generous donation to a
woman with a great community chest, or to
repay your next-door neighbor for turning down
his stereo.

> *Note: For certain college courses, using sex to
> avoid an "incomplete" may not be sanctioned.
> See your bursar.*

Entertainment 70
To fend off boredom if you're on your
honeymoon, it's raining, there's nothing good
on television, and your husband went down
the hall for ice three hours ago and hasn't
returned. Also an amusing diversion while
driving across Texas. (Don't forget: Buckle up.)

HOW EATING THE PROPER FOODS CAN HELP YOUR SEX LIFE

FOOD	SOURCE	APPLICATION
Chili	Mexico, diners named Mom's, the ICU of marginal HMO hospitals	Increases confidence if you have sex with any person other than yourself.
Apples	Trees	Build sturdier elbows, whiter and more seductive teeth, keep colon in mint condition.
Kelp	The Pacific Ocean, Lake Ontario	Reduces lust during PTA meetings, controls prurient thoughts during Lent.

FOOD	SOURCE	APPLICATION
Brownies	Bakeries and your neighbor's windowsill	Speed recovery from morning sex, enable immediate operation of coffeemaker.
Garlic	Rome	Repels aggressive flashers.
Goo Goo Clusters	Nashville, Tennessee	Diminish guilt over too much sex.
Milky Way	Everywhere	Diminishes pain when you have too little sex.
Minestrone	Italian mothers	Allows you to cope with any blind date who picks you up in her tractor.
Bagels	Israel	Good for biting down on when pleasure becomes too intense.

FOOD	SOURCE	APPLICATION
Tacos	Southern Israel	Lessen erotic thoughts during Purim and peace conferences.
Barbecue	Picnics, weddings alfresco, tennis camp	Ensures simultaneous orgasms even if both partners are not in same bed.
Wine (red)	Grapes	Healthy heart, happy demeanor, inhibits gag reflex during oral sex with a partner dressed as Elvis.
Hot fudge sundae	Your kitchen	Privacy. Give to the kids so they stay downstairs while you and hubby have a tryst.

HOW TO EAT
IN BED

Sex making you hungry? Dieting lovers will be happy to learn that, according to statistics, eating in bed is ten times safer than smoking in bed. We do suggest, however, taking the following precautions:

1. Avoid "light" foods like alfalfa and tea. Not only do they offer little in the way of nourishment, but they are not "fun" foods, like Sara Lee or figs.

2. For now, concentrate on the heavier, but not too heavy, foods that stay in your body longer (in the case of Hamburger Helper, seventeen months) and provide sustenance should you decide that a weekend of marathon sex is better than shopping for a couch. Our suggestions:

FOOD	WILL SUSTAIN YOU FOR
Sushi (12 pieces)	19 minutes
Gnocchi	11 days
Southern fried chicken:	
Georgia	10 hours
South Carolina	11 hours
Miami	15 hours
Chopped liver	1 week
Potato salad (German is best)	5 hours
Fried dumplings:	
Regular	2 days
The kind your aunt makes	9 weeks
Strudel:	
Light, flaky crust	9 hours
The kind Grandma made	9 weeks

3. Avoid delicacies that shed. According to
   the AMA, next to potato chips and dried
   prune flecks, muffin crumbs and peanut
   shells are the leading cause of bedsores.

4. Stay with "carefree" foods. Having to shuck oysters or skin a coconut during arousal can kill the mood.

5. Don't avail yourselves of items subject to spillage. Borscht, gazpacho, hot coffee, and won ton soup are good examples.

6. Keep legs firmly crossed at all times. Ignore this advice and the male partner's eyes will bulge should the entire top of a steaming pizza suddenly plunge into his lap.

7. Chinese food is a best bet, since MSG has been found to be effective in heightening the senses and alleviating the more extreme forms of fetishism (for example, inability to fully enjoy sex unless wearing a cape). Avoid fried rice, however, as it tends to get stuck among chest hairs and must be removed with tweezers or waxing.

8. Never moan while gnawing on pepperoni.

9. Wiping greasy hands on a loving partner is a no-no.

HOW TO ORDER IN

Dieting lovers can easily survive on nothing but sex, jambalaya, and a multivitamin for up to six hours, possibly eight with macaroons. Those, however, who fear they are losing too much weight too quickly, but are too tired to walk to the kitchen can opt for ordering in. Some guidelines:

1. When to order in? Ideally, before you begin sexual activity or, if lovemaking is already in progress, after foreplay, thus giving you something to chew on during intercourse.

2. Who decides what to order? Who wears the pants in the family? You? Your partner? Her mother? If you've not yet "tied the knot," joint decisions are best. Should a conflict arise (such as shredded pork with bean sauce versus ten burritos), the lover who is (a) hungriest or (b) bitchiest decides.

3. Who makes the call? The partner who (a) speaks most distinctly and (b) has the most patience, should the person taking the order speak a romance language only (Chinese or Northern Mexican, for example).

4. Who answers the door? The person who, at the moment the doorbell rings, is (a) wearing the most clothing and (b) is not in the throes of orgasm. Alternatively, ask the delivery person to simply hand the container in through the bedroom window. Note: Asking delivery person to "join in" is considered kinky in Ohio.

5. Who pays? Usually the male partner, although in some cases it is the person who earns the most (after taxes).

6. If you do decide to go out instead, good sex should leave you too weak to pick up a check.

Food Fight Advisory: A fun way to determine who gets the good side of the bed (that's the side closest to the kitchen) after sex.

IMPORTANT LIFE EVENTS: HOW LONG AFTERWARD SHOULD YOU WAIT TO HAVE SEX?

AFTER	YOU SHOULD WAIT
Dinner	30 minutes
Your mother-in-law finally moves out	8 seconds
Getting downsized	1 week
Receiving a promotion	1 minute
Circumcision	A very long time
Meeting the love of your life (Five minutes, if "love of your life" feels the same way.)	5 dates
Divorce:	
Your idea	1 week
Spouse's idea	10 minutes
Hip replacement	2 weeks

Having your nails done	5 hours
Sunday Mass	3 hours
Wedding:	
Yours	6–7 hours
Your ex's	2 minutes

Release from federal penitentiary .... 2 hours
(Five hours if you were having sex while
behind bars. See Federal Penal Code,
section 559: Statutes pertaining to conjugal
visits with spouse, significant other, or a
wanton guard.)

WHAT A MAN
REALLY WANTS
IN A WOMAN

THE IDEAL FEMALE PARTNER:

- Does it on the first date.

- Never asks, "Am I the best?"—she knows she is.

- Doesn't mind if, through no fault of her own, he gives her multiple orgasms.

- Doesn't complain if her pulchritude (sensuous lips, ample bosom, great legs) causes him to experience a teensy premature orgasm (while having his fortune told, for example).

- Never combines sex with a manicure (unless her partner is a multitasker).

- Doesn't have a cat.

- Has a cat but it's stuffed.

- Keeps a well-stocked refrigerator next to the bed.

- Can improvise if his back goes out.

- Always calls out the right name no matter how hot the sex.

- Never wears curlers to bed, unless they also pull in a local radio station.

- Makes lots of noise.

- But not enough noise to scare (a) the neighbors or (b) his roommate.

- Has great health insurance (including prescription drug coverage!).

WHAT A WOMAN REALLY WANTS IN A MAN

THE IDEAL MALE PARTNER:

- Takes direction well.
- Helps out with the rent.
- Is not put off by the "Objects may appear larger than they actually are" label on her bra.
- Respects her in the morning.
- Asks, "Am I the best?" only if he knows the answer.
- Never cheats (that is, fakes orgasm), unless he has theater tickets.
- Has a formidable sexual technique (the lover who can churn butter with the tip of his tongue can write his own ticket).
- Lets her keep her nightie on during sex if she feels a draft . . . or is modest.
- Doesn't shout "Fore!" at the moment of orgasm.

- Lasts a reasonable time before his orgasm (June).
- Recovers quickly so he can satisfy her again.
- Respects those postcoital urges to shop.
- Gives a to-die-for foot massage.
- Waits until after sex to turn on Fox News.
- Separates whites from colors.

21 STEPS TO BECOMING A GREAT LOVER

Tips from our panel of cuddly dieters:

1. Become an amazing dancer. (Does *your* health club offer affordable tango lessons?)

2. Strengthen your forearms. They'll be of service when giving a deserving partner a long, luxurious Swedish (or Turkish) massage.

3. Know where to buy wholesale.

4. Learn to play Chopin.

5. Be supportive—type your partner's résumé.

6. If it has been a rough day, be considerate: Help your partner lie down.

7. On cold nights, keep your partner warm. No chest hair? Wear a sexy cardigan.

8. Keep your erogenous zones in working order. Between lovers? Practice with a friend.

9. Gratitude is everything. If sex was wondrous, send flowers (two dozen yellow roses if it was extraordinary).

10. Self-esteem is everything: If you've engaged in self-pleasuring, send yourself flowers (two daisies if it was extraordinary).

11. Light candles (or a nightlight if you're allergic to wax).

12. Be responsive when your partner says, "Don't stop now," "Don't stop yet," and "It's for you."

13. Never moan in a monotone; you'll sound mentally challenged.

14. Cultivate a wicked sense of humor. (You may need it when you taste her bean sprout casserole.)

15. Think of a bubble bath for two with champagne as romance on the high seas.

16. An aura of mystery is sexy. If you're at a business convention, remove your name tag before making love.

17. Be charming (charm school scholarships available from NOW).

18. Learn to make blueberry waffles.

19. Instead of going, "eew!," tell your partner that foot fungus fascinates you.

20. Remember: lust is good—it raises testosterone levels by 3 feet.

21. Wait until *after* sex to put on your shoes.

SEXUAL ACCESSORIES NO LOVER SHOULD BE WITHOUT

(TO ENHANCE THE EROTIC EXPERIENCE AND MAKE IT MORE MEMORABLE)

- Starting gun. Sets the mood, scares away mice if you live above a pet store.

- Shredder. For shredding (1) incriminating love notes and (2) used-up lovers.

- Lap counter. Helpful for determining the size of your lover's lap.

- Stopwatch. If you've been having some last-minute sex, use watch to time her contractions.

- Blood pressure monitor. Essential for lovers residing in an assisted living facility.

- Stethoscope. See above.

- Flashlight. For those all-important face-checks—to see if partner is smiling or grimacing. After sex, use to find partner's retainer.

- Chewing gum. Calms nerves, keeps breath minty fresh if your gums are shot.
- Sponge. Obvious.
- Sponge cake. More absorbent than an ordinary sponge.
- Aphrodisiac. Too many to name here, but you can't go wrong with caviar or a digestive aid like pork chops.*
- An Oscar. For a partner who says, "I never did *that* before" convincingly.
- Birth control. Most effective: A grandmother rocking back and forth in the corner saying, "Don't mind me."
- Hourglass. For taking partner's pulse.
- Bidet. For rinsing the salad.

*All calorie counts negotiable.

III.
PREPARING
FOR YOUR
PARTNER

An hour with a great lover will have the same effect as a week on a diet.

—GIUSEPPI CREDENZA, PASTRY CHEF

The road to perfect sex begins with a perfect you. In addition to showing how much weight you lose while getting ready for your partner, we want to ensure you are physically and mentally up to even the most grueling sexual activity. To guide and reassure you, we list below the questions most often asked by people about to, or think they are about to, have sex. (Note for the insecure: Most fears are groundless.)

- Why am I doing this?

- How's my stamina?

- When does the Viagra kick in? ("How should I know?" is not a romantic answer.)

- Can I gallantly carry my partner into the bedroom without toppling over?

- Will my partner adore my pores?

- Can I discreetly pop that last-minute zit?

- How are my toenails?

- Is it anxiety or an arrhythmia?

- Should we undress now, or after sex?

- Will it be fun?

- Will it be meaningful?

- If it's meaningful will it still be fun?

- Why are her sheets autographed?

- Will I hate myself in the morning? Or after lunch?

PHYSICAL CONDITIONING

A sound mind in a fat body slips around.

—SIR TITO FARTSEK, PH.D.

During sex our body does wondrous things. We grab and grope, we slide and squirm, sometimes we bounce, all the while performing feats of agility usually reserved for last-minute Christmas shopping. Yet, instead of preparing ourselves, most of us just jump into bed without stretching, touching the toes, or spending even a few quiet moments doing tai chi.

Unfortunately, inadequate preparation can lead to premature exhaustion (while doing a crossword puzzle, for example), the signs of which include shortness of breath, dizziness if you lie down too fast, and an inability to chew inexpensive cuts of meat. Additionally, the habitually sedentary man (a fifty-year-old software programmer who sweats only during chess tournaments) who suddenly "gets lucky" (a Libyan cocktail waitress* seeking her green card, for instance) and is called upon to "exercise" may experience shin splints, rendering him incapable of visiting the mall and making more than seven trips to the Chinese buffet. Furthermore, the President's Council on Physical Fitness, in its landmark "No Child's Left Behind" study, suggests that a need to nap after heavy exertion such as taking a power nap, accepting an award, or making a seafood gumbo indicates that one's condition may not be tip-top.

The following modest exercises are designed to help even the most out-of-shape build enough stamina to cope with any partner, even a suburban divorcée whose last sexual encounter coincided with the fall of the Berlin Wall.

Good Samaritan Tip: Even at its shallowest, sex is usually more satisfying than helping a little old lady cross the street.

*Country has been changed to protect the innocent.

LE WARM-UP

Perform the exercise of your choice at least one hour before sex. Remember to breathe through your nose or, if it's stuffed, your partner's nose.

ACTIVITY	CALORIES BURNED

Push-ups (5) 55
Firms upper arms and shoulders, provides strength to hold on during extra-intricate maneuvers (the Heimlich, for instance) and to lift a partner who has fallen asleep on top of you.

Sit-ups (7) 49
Tones vital stomach muscles, enabling you to quickly leap out of bed should you hear the bells of an ice cream truck.

Reverse sit-ups (3) 549
For super strength. Do exactly what you do for a regular sit-up except lie facedown on the floor. Shag carpet a must.

Touch toes (10) 33
Increases flexibility, allows you to try positions
that would normally damage your spine and
turn you into a beggar. Also lets you reach for
snacks, as well as sedatives.

Touch waist (10) 6
For those not yet sufficiently limber to reach
their toes. Similar effect as above, but less,
far less.

Arm curls (20) 77
Builds strong biceps necessary for carrying
a full-size partner either into the bedroom or
out of a White Castle. Also makes tattoo more
prominent and provides brute strength needed
after dynamic sex to lift mattress and replace
a broken bed slat.

Squeezing a rubber ball (20 squeezes) 8
During sex, a strong grip is needed for
everything from picking up fruit to, if he has to
be walked, tossing the dog out the window. It is
especially vital for clinging to your partner
should the bed capsize.

Jogging (at least 1 mile) 110
The ultimate all-around exercise for increasing stamina. Enlarges lung capacity, thereby permitting, during sex, moaning in a variety of languages and holding your breath for several hours if you think you hear a burglar downstairs.

For the nonathletic, there are alternate methods of achieving erotic fitness. They include vigorous activities such as laps in the wading pool, checkers, and crossing your living room in a balloon.

MENTAL CONDITIONING

It is impossible to enjoy sex if depressed or not in the mood, or if the mind is distracted by everyday cares. For now, you must strive for a feeling of well-being; worries about the economy, the environment, overdue bills, and your teeth must be put aside until you have either sex or your daily drink, whichever comes first. Some proven methods of dissipating tension while achieving serenity:

ACTIVITY	CALORIES BURNED
Transcendental meditation	4
Incidental meditation (if you eat lunch at your desk)	6
Self-hypnosis	9
Seeing your therapist (per session)	22
If therapist makes house calls	9
As long as you make her dinner	30

Biofoodback 23
Compulsively watching TV cooking shows until
you achieve enlightenment and realize that
baking an olive and rosemary country bread
is a form of foreplay.

PRIMPING (HER)

H

ard work, but worth it.

ACTIVITY	CALORIES BURNED
Tweezing stray facial hairs	3
Pruning eyebrows:	18
Using hedge trimmer	175
Applying false eyelashes	15
While head-bobbing to:	
Janet Jackson	2
Hip-hop	118
Seasickness	1,266
Assembling that just-right outfit:	30
One that makes you look extra hot	49
One that your partner can remove easily	5

GROOMING (HIM)

Hard work, but worth it.

ACTIVITY	CALORIES BURNED
Sucking in	24
Turning blue	124

IV. SETTING THE SCENE

Begin with a romantic setting, one that makes your lover hope—unless (a) your air conditioner broke or (b) you have cramps—that the night will never end.

Start with an examination of the bathroom. Does it sparkle? Is there a new cake of soap in the sink, or that pathetic chip of Ivory you've been hoarding until payday? Then the kitchen: Make sure the refrigerator's stocked—snack-deprived lovers get testy. If you hate washing dishes, can you eat beef Stroganoff off the floor? And a microwave can't hurt. Popcorn is lover-friendly and low in calories, and you can really get to know each other by flossing those annoying little specks from between each other's teeth (using the same piece of floss for both of you is unlawful unless you're engaged, or related). And, of course, the bedroom. Do soiled socks litter the floor? Is it too late to buy a new mattress? If you have lots of disposable income, strew the bed with orchids, making sure they don't clash with the 134 stuffed animals already there. Change the sheets, fluff the pillows, and, if your last partner was partial to gel, change the pillowcases. Check under the bed. Dust balls, crumpled tissues, and a dozing ex will repulse a finicky partner.

Finally, be considerate: Is there sufficient reading matter to occupy your partner should you take too long (a) in the bathroom or (b) to climax? (Studies show that many alpha males, while waiting for a lover to "prettify" herself in the bathroom, have actually gotten their pilot's license.)

BATHROOM BASICS: SEVEN THINGS A NEW LOVER SHOULD NEVER SEE IN YOUR MEDICINE CABINET

1. Prozac

2. Half a cigar

3. Anything labeled "stool softener"

4. Rogaine

5. Bunion shields

6. Preparation H

7. Live ammunition

PREPARING
THE BEDROOM

ACTIVITY	**CALORIES BURNED**

If you're fussy 111
(Give or take 3 calories.)

Includes dusting, plumping the pillows, cuing
up the right music, checking for mattress
failure, and, if your partner's a patriot, affixing
a flag decal either to the headboard or, if
partner is a super patriot, your forehead. Make
sure the lighting is right. Too dark and the
place becomes a coal mine; too light and it
looks like an operating room (try a hundred tiny
energy-efficient bath candles). Unless you're a
certified swami, avoid incense. Use props such
as books to show what a perfect person you are.
Books of poetry, interspersed with a few comic
books, convey literacy and versatility. They
should be conspicuously placed—on the dresser
and the night table, and perhaps one or two
under the covers. Also select a few books that
give the impression that you are unusual—
slightly eccentric but not (yet) certifiable—thus
adding to the mystery of the sexual experience.
A few suggested titles: *Lord of the Rungs:*

The Man Who Made Ladders Fun; *The Joy of Sax: A Hepcat Tells All*; *Precious Flank Steak: Secrets of a PETA Fanatic Turned Butcher*; and, if you're into haiku, *Jingles of the Japanese*. And, last, tune the TV (sound muted) to the Discovery Channel—rather than QVC and two eerie women selling "Youth Enhancing Crème, 8 ounces only $499.99 plus $100 shipping"— to show you're not a ditz.

Note: If someone extra special is coming over, you may want to change the sheets or, if that's not an option, at least flip them over. Add 22 calories if they're heavy sheets.

THE WELL-APPOINTED BEDROOM

everal of the more outspoken dieters on our panel actually had a fistfight over whether the focal point of the room should be a treadmill or a scale. We tend to think that such items, while helpful, detract from the overall romantic effect so sought by passionate couples. Hence these suggestions, which can also be beneficial to nondieting lovers seeking an idyllic retreat from the cares of the day.

1. Candles. Not only intimate but, if scented, can mask the smell of fear often emanating from the male dieter whose partner is either (a) overly aggressive or (b) an intern. (Bonus: Scented candles also attract a better class of moth.)

2. Mirror on the ceiling. A reliable way for the female partner to check (a) for spinach between her teeth and (b) her makeup.

Also enables a suspicious female, when on the bottom, to see if her partner frosts his back hair.

3. A "Choking Victim" poster above the bed—not only decorative but indicates that oral sex is welcome.

4. Bifocals. To read "Choking Victim" poster.

5. Satin sheets. More sensuous than Astroturf, plus easier to launder. During extra-passionate moments, couples may lose control, slide off the bed, and find themselves on their neighbor's patio. Don't forget to say hello.

6. Stopwatch. As noted previously: Essential for couples trying to (a) finish in time for *Matlock* reruns and (b) achieve their target heart rate. Indispensable if partner charges by the hour.

7. All-purpose snack. For energy we recommend either gherkins or a Power Bar, and, for its anticoagulant properties, may we sing the praises of last Yule's fruitcake?

8. Dirt Devil. The preferred "sex toy" for vacuuming the chest of the partner addicted to Pringles or trail mix.

9. Dental mirror. With dieters reluctant to flaunt their sexuality, locating that G spot can take months. The reflective device of choice for finding it.

10. Cattle prod. Low setting is useful for expressing displeasure with a partner who, immediately after sex, rolls over and falls asleep. Use high setting for the partner who, immediately after sex, rolls over and calls his wife.

11. Computer terminal. Enables the lover on top to lean over and check the new Web site for hits.

12. Ivy on the walls. Eases erectile difficulties in lovers who flunked out of Harvard.

13. Box of tissues. After sex, shedding tears of gratitude for a job well done is not uncommon.

14. Instant replay. A video camera for studying your mistakes is nice.

15. Confetti. To celebrate a simultaneous "We did it!" orgasm.

NEW AGE ADVISORY

Feng Shui our bedroom? Spiritual couples believe it lowers stress, increases weight loss, and releases secret sexual energies imprisoned in your underwear.* Suggestions from Dagmar, our certified Feng Shui expert:

1. The bed. Ringing sacred bells (two tinkle-tinkles work best) will banish negativity caused by decorator sheets that might have been woven in sweatshops by Balinese asthmatics.

2. The male. In addition to raising his sperm count, orienting the male partner along southeast magnetic lines of force enables him to draw sexual power from the mattress while maintaining his sense of humor should you inadvertently call out the wrong name during sex. (Example: If you moan, "Pepe, oh, Pepe," and his name is Doodles.)

*It also makes reincarnation go smoothly should you die during sex.

3. Erotic clapping. Dispels negative energies—effective if the male partner is impotent, and "Mazel tov" isn't working. Use the special Baghavit-Cincinnati clapping technique: Several short, emotionally centered claps around the "lazy organ" will drive out "nonvirile" energies caused by either a diet high in salt or too much beer. Note: If clapping fails, take a plant mister and spritz the organ with holy chi water.

4. Emergency clapping. Similar to the above—use only if you suddenly get a leg cramp or see something you really want on eBay.

5. Birth control. Picture yourselves in a protective shield of white light.

THE WELL-
APPOINTED
BATHROOM

Even under everyday circumstances, the bathroom should be regarded as a holy place, a sanctuary for cleansing the body, renewing the spirit, and, if kitty litter's under the sink, watching your cat *kvell*. During sex, the bathroom also becomes a first aid station, a place for private mid-sex touch-ups. It should therefore be spotless, shining, and filled with amenities such as soft, fluffy, low-mileage towels, a cheerful, nonmossy shower curtain, a new bar of soap, preferably with a muted aroma, an extra toothbrush, and a toilet that flushes with a satisfying and reassuring whoosh. If possible, we suggest boiling the entire bathroom, just to be certain. If this is not convenient, try the following:

ACTIVITY	CALORIES BURNED

Erasing two-month-old ring from tub 122

Scrubbing (de-crudding) tiles 431

Removing alien vegetation
(such as a victory garden)
from shower curtain 1,800

Replacing all towels:

    From Bed, Bath & Beyond 10

    From motel with hourly rates 30

Chiseling away excessive
soap buildup in soap dish 8

Tuning the exhaust fan 57

*Anxiety Advisory: If you have one of those
"water-saver" toilets requiring twenty-two
flushes to kill a Q-tip, consider going to your
partner's place, especially if you're bulimic.*

THE ESSENTIALS: ADDITIONAL LAST-MINUTE PREPARATIONS

ACTIVITY	CALORIES BURNED
Vacuuming	24
Hiding Cliffs Notes sex manual (Okay to write answers on your palm.)	15
Getting rid of:	
The ratty slippers	10
The photo of you and your ex in a hot tub	22
Your "Stamp Collector of the Year" trophy (It's just not sexy.)	12
Your roommate	1,006
Putting answering machine on mute	9
Dimming the lights:	
For the ambience	6

ACTIVITY	CALORIES BURNED

Lighting candles:

    For intimacy 6

    For warmth 14

    To conceal the smell of kitty litter 10

Affixing "Thank you for not smoking"
notice to headboard 11

*Note: Women who like things their way can
hang a large oil painting of Karl Marx on the
wall, admonishing visitors to "Please put the
seat down."*

SEX AT HIS PLACE

The first time she stays at his place, unless she's fearless, or naive, the savvy woman takes responsibility for her creature comforts, as noted below.

RESPONSIBILITY	HIS	HERS
Indoor plumbing	•	
New toothbrush		•
Birth control:		
Diaphragm		•
12 vodka gimlets	•	
Dainty his 'n' her washcloths		•
Hair dryer (He may have one from a leftover girlfriend, but why take a chance?)		•
Clean sheets	•	
Clean decorator sheets		•
Toilet tissue, fresh roll	•	
Lint remover (No man in his right mind admits to owning a lint remover.)		•

RESPONSIBILITY	HIS	HERS
Your therapist's photo (If you get nervous, gives you that "I'm in strange surroundings" sense of security.)		•
Place card for each pillow (Romantic touch.)		•
Little flashlight (To help you find your way to the bathroom in the dark.)	•	
Breakfast (Ideally, in your honor, he will have purchased wonderful things like pancake mix, blueberries, eggs, bacon, and Cocoa Pebbles, all supplemented with freshly ground coffee. But just in case, it can't hurt to have a jar of Ovaltine and some fiber in your purse.)	•	
Passport (In case he wants to take you to Rome for the weekend.)		•
Pre-nup (In case things get serious.)		•
Booties (In case you get cold feet.)	•	

CONDOMS, THE PURCHASE OF

Just standing before the "Family Planning Center" at the drugstore or your local Hummer dealership, trying to be an informed consumer and decide which condom is appropriate, can burn more calories than a week at chess camp, especially if, when you pay, the cashier has a "look who thinks they're getting lucky" smirk (okay to wipe it off with a polo mallet). A few survival strategies:

ACTIVITY	CALORIES BURNED
Putting on disguise:	
Sunglasses	4
A tribal mask	17
Considering the choices	11
Trying to appear nonchalant	22
Whistling a happy tune	30

ACTIVITY	CALORIES BURNED

Making your selection:

If you're totally uninhibited 4

Painfully self-conscious 202

Underage 792

Asking advice from sales associate 17

Who turns out to be your
guidance counselor 285

Coping with embarrassment 394
(Cashier brandishes your ten-pack* and
screams, "How much for the reservoir tips?")

Getting fitted 150

No fitting room 300

*Note: In an emergency, okay to use
a Ziploc bag.*

*It is the wise and optimistic lover who buys in bulk.

CREATING A DIVERSION:

Condom-buying strategies for those:

1. Who live in a small town.

2. Whose ID is shaky.*

Purchase of various "decoy" items:

Aspirin	9
Mother's Day card	14
Bathroom scale	45
Tums	5
Cough drops	6
Magazine (*The Economist* is good)	12
Codeine	25
Without a prescription	100
Fleet disposable enema	148
Cane with ergonomic handle	216

Condom No-no: Unless the label says otherwise, condoms are not dishwasher safe.

*Reputable stores will not sell such items to anyone under twelve years of age.

AVOIDING SEX WITHOUT HURTING PARTNER'S FEELINGS

ACTIVITY	CARB GRAMS BURNED
Faking:	
Headache	14
Cluster headache	42
Migraine	233
Sleep	7
Insomnia	90
Nausea	28
Business trip	500

Romance Advisory: Worst excuse for not having sex with one's spouse: "You looked so perfect lying there, I couldn't bear to disturb you."

WEIGHT LOSS BONUS #3: WHEN IS IT APPROPRIATE TO HAVE SEX?

After five dates? Ten dates? Before your roommate gets home? Right after sex education class? As soon as it gets dark? So many choices, but remember: Because your date brought you flowers, paid for dinner and the movie, treated you to popcorn, and detailed your car does not mean you're obligated to have sex . . . or even grant a goodnight kiss. An overview:

ACTIVITY	CARB GRAMS BURNED
Waiting until marriage:	
If neither partner believes in premarital sex	40
But their hormones are raging	2,849
Having sex after marriage:	
Immediately (on the receiving line)	1,893
The honeymoon	745
The first grandchild	18

DURING SEX

V. INITIAL INTIMACIES

You're through preparing—it's time to get physical. Your partner's references check out, the question of "Your place or mine?" has been resolved (generally the partner with either the best address—terrace with ocean view—or the fewest dirty dishes in the sink plays host). Even if you desperately want each other, however, take your time. Slowly removing each other's clothes and folding them neatly (especially if you're still at the restaurant) burns far more calories than simply tearing them off and diving into bed. Instead, once you're home, sitting on the couch, quietly holding hands, staring into each other's eyes and discussing the Hirschhorn Amendment (in your underwear) will, when you finally make love, make it that much better.

GETTING YOUR PARTNER IN THE MOOD

High-calorie approaches, other than video games, that never fail:

ACTIVITY	CALORIES BURNED
Reading romantic poetry to each other:	
Shelley (Percy Bysshe)	5
Lord Byron	6
Browning	8
Blake*	15
One immaculate Shakespeare sonnet	20
(Romance experts cite CIX: "O! Never say that I was false of heart" as killer stuff, unless recited with a southern accent.)	
Reading steamy passages from *The Brothers Karamazov*	½

*Irresistible to women who went to Smith.

ACTIVITY	CALORIES BURNED

Ice breakers if your partner's a bit reserved:

Whoopie cushion 11

Squirting flower 14

Joy buzzer 10

Exploding goat 20

Reading ribald excerpts from:

Balzac 23

The Marquis de Sade 44

The Congressional Record 507

Humming spirituals 119

Listening to music:

Light classical 3

Heavy classical 7

Opera:

Mozart 17

Wagner 222

Gershwin 21

Contemporary Christian 95
(Or klezmer if you're on a kibbutz.)

You singing:

Dancing:

(4-calorie penalty if you eat the rose.)

(Not recommended if you met your new
partner at a church social. Begin with
something artistic, like *Debbie Does Kenosha*
[the director's cut], which won an Oscar, an
Emmy, and the Pillsbury Bakeoff.)

*Flab Check Alert: Dancing close allows you a
sneak preview of your partner's body tone; you
can then decide if you wish to go further. Great
pecs can make up for a mushy back, and a high
behind can compensate for a low IQ.*

COMMUNICATING

Naturally, the shorter and less imaginative the conversation, the less energy used and the fewer calories burned. Beginning a conversation with "I've got nothing to talk about, let's rent a room," though certainly direct, will likely alienate even the most willing partner unless you're granted points for candor.

Suggestions:

TOPIC	CALORIES BURNED
Eggnog: Enchanting holiday elixir or hideous concoction?	9
How you despise materialistic people	16
Your jewelry size	20
How you are striving to become your own person	152
And become less dependent on your personal shopper	162
The curse of split ends	9
The glories of Irish heavy metal	110
Pleats: Yes or no?	30

*Boredom Alert: You may be boring the person
you're desperately trying to impress if she uses
your hand to stifle her yawns. Perk things up
either by changing the subject or playing
Russian Roulette.*

INITIATING SEXUAL ACTIVITY

ACTIVITY	CALORIES BURNED
Sitting on partner's lap	11
Sitting on partner's laptop	245
Giving secret signal (Such as removing shoulder holster.)	5
Breathing hard	11
Scrawling message on bedroom mirror:	
"I want you now!"	22
"Mirror, mirror, on the wall, who is fairest of them all?"	44
If partner is illiterate	3
Playing doctor:	
Gynecologist	31
Sports medicine	60
Playing dentist	12

MAKING THAT FIRST MOVE

ACTIVITY	CALORIES BURNED
If you are shy	141
If you sell used cars	2
If you fear:	
Success	33
Humiliation	80
If you are easily intimidated when a person acts distant and reserved	41

Tip: A person who orders you to "keep your hands to yourself" is acting distant and reserved.

If you have an inferiority complex the size of Guam	600
Nonchalantly asking partner if it's okay to put your arm around him/her	3
Dislocating shoulder	295
Acting cool	8
Pouncing	204

FEAR OF REJECTION

ACTIVITY	CALORIES BURNED
If you are a:	
Bed wetter	99
Telemarketer	0
Overcoming fear with:	
Courage	33
Determination	38
Motivational tape*	52
Nature's own remedy (alcohol)	1
Last resort:	
Begging	10
Black magic	40
Money	5

Workout Note: The timid lover will burn extra calories with a partner whose thigh has a tattoo proclaiming, "If you can read this, you're too damn close."

*Uncool to ask partner to wait while you go in the next room to spend forty-five minutes listening to the tape.

BODY CONTACT AND INITIAL TOUCHING

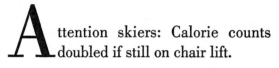

ttention skiers: Calorie counts doubled if still on chair lift.

ACTIVITY	CALORIES BURNED
Fumbling	4
Casually rummaging around	7

Petting:

Above the waist under loose-fitting garment such as sweater, T-shirt, or shower curtain 21

Below the waist under tight ski pants ... 46
(Stop if you suddenly lose feeling in your wrist.)

Gentle stroking	10
Fondling (per fondle)	6
Neck rub	12

Back rub:

Regular 15

Full-service 22

Complete body oil massage 33

Hands-free 188

KISSING

ACTIVITY	CALORIES BURNED
Puckering up	3½
Gentle	10
Heavy	18
Heavy breathing (windows fogging)	26
Fervent	135

(Examples: Giving partner's shirt collar a hickey, or actually nibbling on partner's uvula.)

French kiss (teeth open, lips apart)	25
British kiss (teeth clenched, lips apart)	19
German kiss (everything clenched)	130
American (teeth open, lips apart, tongues frantically dueling for the Tic Tac)	142

Moisture Note: When kissing, an expert lover understands the difference between the exquisitely moist and the great mashing slobbering kiss that saturates the entire face and causes the victim to utter, "Eew!"

REMOVING CLOTHES (AT LAST!)

ACTIVITY	CALORIES BURNED
With partner's consent*	12
Without partner's consent	187
In winter	72
(Parka, flannel shirt, pants, watch cap, earmuffs, scarf, gloves, long underwear, socks, boots, and combination pager–handwarmer.)	
In summer	3
Removing socks by violently shaking feet	418
Unhooking power bra (theft-proof catch):	
Using two calm hands	7
Using one very dexterous hand	44
(Advanced lovers only.)	
Using two trembling hands	67
If she doesn't help	753

*Assess a 25-calorie bonus if he can remove your Sid Vicious T-shirt without disturbing your cowboy hat.

LEARNED
DISCUSSION

Should you remove all of your clothes?* The answer is generally yes. It frees those crucial pheromones, and, more important, your partner will take it as a sign (a) of commitment and (b) that you've been working out. Women are especially put off by men who, unaware that sex is a full-contact sport, won't make love unless wearing shorts proclaiming, "Home of the whopper!" There are also lovers who need their lucky charm—the recovering chain smoker, for example, who can only have sex while stroking his nicotine patch, and certain women who can't climax unless clutching a canasta deck. It is, however, generally acceptable to wear adornments such as earrings, rings, discreet religious symbols, and campaign buttons.

*The impact of seeing one's partner naked varies. Some women, if they like what they see, turn up the lights. Some men, if they love what they see, suddenly believe in marriage.

Once undressed, no need to worry about those few extra pounds:

- They're difficult to see by candlelight;
- They're even more difficult to see by moonlight; and
- Most lovers look thinner when they're lying down.

THE JUICY DETAILS

Diet researchers at the CIA's Passion Foundation tell us that every part of a lover's body is acutely sensitive to a well-executed kiss, especially if the subject (a) is ticklish and (b) fidgets. Dieters will be astonished to learn the calories consumed when a consummate lover who has no fear of germs kisses any or (better) all of the following areas:

KISSING	CALORIES BURNED
Eyelid	3
Forehead	11
Earlobe	21
(Double when performed by a partner with an overbite who uses the Shiatsu-Bernstein* technique.)	
Neck	29
Little bonus bites (per bite)	6
Breasts	574
(Deduct 564 calories if surgically enhanced.)	

*Some names have been changed.

AROUSAL AND STIMULATION: THE BASICS

It was difficult to assign caloric values for this category—what is megawatt sex for some may be boredom to others. One person, for instance, may respond sexually to a pot roast; another, less sensual person may eat it. And there are those who do not consider the phrase "free valet parking" sexual. Hence we freely admit that counts below are somewhat imprecise.

ACTIVITY	CALORIES BURNED
Blowing in partner's ear (can release up to 3 quarts of estrogen if partner super-responsive):	
Using lips 9	
Using bellows 115	
Using leaf blower* 290	
Blowing in your own ear . . . . 155 (Experimental form of autoeroticism still being tested.)	

*Do not try this at home.

WEIGHT LOSS BONUS #4: DO YOU LIKE WHAT YOU SEE?

ACTIVITY	CARB GRAMS BURNED

Striptease (her) 87

If you are even marginally graceful, stripping to music presents an excellent opportunity to arouse an appreciative partner and perk up your cabaret act. It also presents the chance to carefully remove your clothes yourself, instead of worrying about the quivering hands of an aroused male desperately trying, though you're still wearing your work boots, to yank off your new Seven jeans. You must be careful, however, not to ruin the amorous mood by attempting something unsuitable that might cause you to look foolish. Pole dancing using the wrong pole (from Krakow instead of Warsaw, for example) not to mention tossing articles of apparel, as you take them off, at your partner and knocking him unconscious with an ankle weight, can be ruinous to the mood.

Striptease (him) 2

When it comes to the promise of sex, the feverish male cares little about niceties. He can, as a matter of fact, go from fully dressed to totally nude in 2.1 seconds; 3 seconds if he's fastidious and pauses to insert shoe trees into his Johnston & Murphys.

HOW TO KEEP A WOMAN WARM

TYPE OF WOMAN	CALORIES BURNED BY HIM
Petite 300	

Teeny-weeny women require the most calories because their own heat-producing apparatus is insufficient—possibly from shivering and constantly picking at salads.

Regular 196	

The average-size woman usually requires just one quilt, leg warmers, and a medium-size male to get her through the night.

Large 89	

Here, the woman's own heat-producing apparatus is fairly efficient. Male need not have a hairy chest and may take periodic breaks from his warming duties to dream and snore.

Abundant 18	

In this case, it is the man who clings to the woman for warmth. In exchange, he brings her her second breakfast, in bed.

WEIGHT LOSS BONUS #5: FEAR

ACTIVITY	CARB GRAMS BURNED
Stage fright	327

Also called "flop sweat." Occurs when both partners are finally naked, the chaperone has left, and it's time to stop stalling and get on with it. (A not unusual wedding-night affliction of honeymooners who do not believe in premarital sex and had an eighteen-year engagement.) Chief symptoms of stage fright include anxiety, wondering why you didn't start your diet sooner, and a need to call Mom. It is easily conquered by locking yourself in the bathroom and releasing "negative internal energies" with a toilet bowl brush.

THE MOMENT OF TRUTH

ACTIVITY	CALORIES BURNED
Lying about your height	14

Having tattoo of ex's name in intimate place:

Breast	22
Bridge of nose	40
With raised lettering	132

Frayed underwear	28

No underwear:

You forgot	9
They fell off	16
Never wear underwear, you're a free spirit	2

Enormous juice stain on shorts (repercussions of a hasty breakfast):

Grapefruit	6
Tomato	53

Holes in socks:

If you are rich	2
If you are poor	120

DISAPPOINTMENT

Clothing can conceal and lie (Who knows what's under that kilt?), and some people may feel disappointed, even cheated, upon seeing their partner naked. In some cases, a less intimate activity may be preferred, such as bagels and cream cheese or bingo. A man who looks fantastic in his Perry Ellis turns out to have shoulders only eight inches wide, a chest like a mouse, and canary legs. A woman removes her shoes and shrinks from 5'7" to 4'9" and no one can find her. Following are some common disappointments and the calories consumed in dealing with them:

SITUATION	CALORIES BURNED
Partner looked better with clothes on	10
Partner looked better with your clothes on	97
Partner looks better with your glasses off	12

Partner's body resembles a
tubercular chicken 138

Partner wearing corrective underwear:

Truss 14

Depends 250

Partner turns out to be the wrong sex 408

You don't mind 7

You don't notice . . . . ½

Botox leaking 70

Typical reactions to sexual disappointment:

ACTIVITY	CALORIES BURNED
Asking for a rain check 8	
Pleading for a rain check 22	
Keeping a stiff upper lip . . . . 3 (Duct tape will keep it from quivering.)	
Going through with it anyway:	
Pity sex 50	
Because you already paid for the motel 66	

Inventing complicated but believable excuse for leaving 75

Examples include:

- "I have to go." (Least complicated.)

- "Forgot my medication."

- "Hear [spouse] blowing the horn."

SHOWERING TOGETHER

Not only a neat way to burn 200 calories (160 calories if you're both under 5'6"), but the sight of a gleaming, lathered body, especially one with great abs and colorful tattoos, is certain to invigorate even the most dormant libido. Since this activity falls into the category of semi-unnatural and deliciously naughty acts, particularly for dieters married twenty-five years or more, we offer these procedural tips:

1. A generous cake of Ivory or, in a pinch, Dove, provides the lather necessary to allow your hands to glide over your partner's body with minimal resistance. Those stingy slivers of soap found in "by the hour" motels do not do the job.

2. This is no time to engage in a power struggle. Because of her delicate skin, selecting water temperature is always the woman's prerogative.

3. Because you're both nude, and unless you promised not to peek, sex in the shower is not inconceivable (although the shorter partner should stand on a phone book).

4. The ethics of using a loofah sensuously— i.e., for purposes other than cleanliness and defoliation—are still being debated. Let your conscience be your guide . . . and watch the navel ring.

5. Men with bad comb-overs and fragile hair weaves should consider either a shower cap or turning the lights off. Discovering that your eight strands of artfully woven hair conceal a major Rogaine failure may cause your partner to fall into a deep and refreshing swoon.

6. Drying each other with a big, fluffy towel is nice, but a blow-dryer's more erotic and, on "low" setting, will dry those bodily niches so susceptible to irritation. (Implant alert: The "high" setting has been known to melt silicone.)

7. Keep the lights low. Not only does this heighten intimacy, it also prevents embarrassing questions if the shower curtain is mildewed or someone's jet-black hair suddenly becomes a strange gray.

Note: If you prefer a romantic bubble bath with little candles around the tub, we suggest a gently aromatic bath powder such as Tranquil Moments, the official bath powder of the California legislature.

GETTING INTO BED

ACTIVITY	CALORIES BURNED

Lifting partner 115
No longer a male-dominated activity. Many a
woman, especially the strong silent type with
a gym membership, will take pride in gently
lifting her man, carrying him into the bedroom,
and lightly tossing him onto the bed. Men,
especially those exhausted from a hard day
of fishing, appreciate this gesture, although
there may be a few who find their manhood
threatened.

Straining 222
(Ask her to put down her purse.)

Turning red 315

Using a dolly 18

Moving aside the 175 Beanie Babies 30

Shivering from:

    Cold sheets 9

    Fear 20

Setting alarm 1

Placing teeth in glass of water 43

(One of our test couples got in and out of bed
137 times before realizing that it couldn't
be done.)

THINGS OFTEN
SAID BEFORE SEX

ACTIVITY	**CALORIES BURNED**

Any sex-related utterance 10

Some typical examples:

- "Do you believe in miracles?"
- "Now I lay me down to sleep."*
- "This little piggy went to market."
- "Race you to the bed."
- "Will I still have to take the final?"
- "Turn your head and cough."
- "Call me Herschel—it gets me hot."

*Sex does not always occur after this particular phrase is uttered.

VI. FOREPLAY

Foreplay is the gateway to pleasure, a time to experiment and try new things, like love bites if you have good teeth.

—DR. TIFFANY DINGLEY,
SEX THERAPIST IN RESIDENCE, WEST POINT

This is where the breathing gets heavy, the heart rate increases, and the pounds start melting away. If you need to use the bathroom, do so now. Those who respond to a partner's "Lord, don't stop now, or even in five minutes" with "Sorry, love, must gargle" should not expect a warm welcome upon returning to bed. (Unstable men find this sort of interruption unsettling and may need ten Paxils to recapture the mood.) The following activities will not just help you lose weight, they also serve to heighten pleasure: Be adventurous. One impotent partner, for instance, achieved remarkable recovery just by watching his girlfriend walk around the room wearing nothing but a welder's mask (he was in construction). And a woman obsessed with gardening actually had a hands-free climax when her lover pressed his lips to her ear and, over and over again, whispered the word "trellis."

And, finally, four things to check for in your lover's bedroom:

1. Sufficient ventilation

2. Fitted sheets

3. Takeout menus

4. A hidden camera

Note: Those pressed for time (working mothers, for example) or who regard foreplay as drudgery may prefer to skip directly to intercourse and hope their partner won't notice.

OUR EXCLUSIVE PREFOREPLAY CHECKLIST

☐ I did go potty so I won't interrupt lovemaking with a "wee wee" emergency.

☐ I've hung a "Do not disturb" sign on the bedroom door (applicable only at motels, or cocktail parties where you and partner are in the bedroom, doing it on the coats).*

☐ (If partner is allergic to animal fur.) I sold the dog and put the cat in her favorite dresser drawer and taped it shut.

☐ Air conditioner adjusted.

☐ Music selected.

☐ Lover's iris scan checks out.

☐ Lighting adjusted to highlight new tongue stud.

☐ Whispered things in lover's ear.

In response, lover:

☐ smiled.

☐ washed my mouth out with soap.

---

*If you're at a motel, be certain the "Do Not Disturb" sign faces out. Displaying the "Please make up the room" or, at cozy inns, the "Please join in" side invites disaster.

HONESTLY TELLING YOUR PARTNER WHAT GETS YOU EXCITED

ACTIVITY	CALORIES BURNED

Level I 115
Pretty much the usual—your basic hugging, kissing, standard foreplay, including massaging the sex manual with baby oil.

Level II 228
A bit more out of the ordinary. May involve a marital aid running on either batteries or hydroelectric power.

Level III 268
Make certain you know your partner well. Covers intimacies using lotions, exotic rubber attire, and wicker furniture. May also include a quick cell call to parents to ask if this is how they had you. Add 10 calories if you let lover say hello.

Level IV 300
Involves any activity in which the phrases
"Buff butt" and "Ursula's passionate lash"
are used. Not recommended if it's only the
second date, and you met in a revival tent.

Coping with response:

Calming horrified partner 365

13 TOP SEXUAL TURNOFFS (FOR HER)

1. Bagpipes.

2. Wedgie.

3. Man insists birth control is woman's responsibility.

4. Klutz (nearly strangled you while "casually" removing your tube top).

5. Refers to his manhood as "the Cookie Monster." (Not funny if it's 5 centimeters long.)

6. Mood killer (love child from his first marriage practicing drums, for example).

7. Painful intercourse (brim of his baseball cap hitting your forehead).

8. Spooky (wants you to tell him a bedtime story).*

---

*If it's *Hansel and Gretel* and he starts to suck his thumb, get out of there.

9. Whisker burn (and inner thighs are starting to smolder).

10. Man's breasts larger than yours.

11. Mullet.

12. Keeps asking you about your past.

13. Pinky ring.

15 TOP SEXUAL TURNOFFS (FOR HIM)

1. Unfashionable (she's wearing last season's burka).

2. Stubborn zipper.

3. Water retention.

4. Killed the mood (asked you to tuck a fifty into her G-string).

5. She's waving the intermediate bondage kit (spurs and a surgical glove).

6. Bounty on her head.

7. Use of ice-cold Mag-Lite to examine vasectomy scar.

8. Michael Jackson bobblehead on her night table.

9. During foreplay partner said, "Wake me when it's over."

10. Pit bull bites (vets suggest morphine in his Mighty Dog).

11. Salary envy (she makes more than you do).*

12. Peanut-size bladder (she used bathroom eight times during foreplay).

13. Keeps asking, "Are you done?"

14. She can pick a buffalo wing clean before you can.

15. Inconsiderate (closed the Murphy bed with you still in it).

*Not a problem if she's your supervisor.

BEING GOOD IN BED: MEN

- Willingly pitches in.
- Shaves.
- Lasts a long time before orgasm.
- Is not distracted by reprimands.
- Does well in at least six different positions.
- Gives partner multiple orgasms.
- Gives himself multiple orgasms (if he deserves it).
- Has a sense of timing that permits simultaneous orgasms with partner.
- Has super sense of timing that permits simultaneous orgasms with couple next door.
- Doesn't keep asking, "How am I doing?"
- Can tell that you like what he's doing.
- Pays special attention to your birthmark.
- Cheerfully gives post- and precoital back rubs.
- Screams and yells only in bed.
- Always removes his watch.
- Can show his "sensitive" feminine side without wearing capri pants.

BEING GOOD IN BED: WOMEN

- Doesn't mind if lover gives her multiple orgasms.
- Lasts only two minutes before first orgasm.
- Keeps a bowl of Junior Mints beside the bed.
- Doesn't wake the neighbors (unless they're light sleepers).
- Enjoys being aggressive.
- Doesn't feel used if partner collapses after four hours of sex.
- Lets partner try anything within reason.
- Doesn't keep asking, "How am I doing?"
- Doesn't keep asking, "How are you doing?"
- Stays awake throughout.
- Is attentive to partner after orgasm.
- Is certified in CPR.
- Has lots of after-sex snacks in her refrigerator.
- Doesn't say, "Poor baby" if man has orgasm while switching off the light.
- Makes the good kind of face during oral sex.

WRITHING

With a skilled partner, can serve as a muscle relaxant if you're stiff, tense, or inhibited.

ACTIVITY	CALORIES BURNED
Writhing from:	
Pleasure	12
Pain	161
Both	240
(Note synergistic effect when combined.)	
Tickling	188
(Add 5 calories if partner holding you down.)	
Something you ate	377
(Add 10 calories if partner holding you up.)	
Additional muscle relaxants:	
Stretching	14
Facial	10
Air guitar	122
Valium	1

TEASING

When done in moderation, teasing your partner with a tongue (preferably yours) or, if your tongue is tired, the dog's, can be highly erotic and a supplemental calorie burner.

ACTIVITY	CALORIES BURNED
Licking partner all over but being careful to avoid any sexually sensitive areas ...... 29 (If partner is hairy, you may find it necessary to floss periodically.)	
Resisting frustrated partner ("You're torturing me!") who is desperately trying to push your head toward a sexually sensitive area 38	
If partner is very athletic 95	

CARESSES

SEXUAL ETHICS

W hat no principled lover should be without. Now is the appropriate time to confess that you:

ACTIVITY	CALORIES BURNED
Still have your virginity:	
Never lost it	20
It grew back	44
Snore	11
But seldom during sex	117
Hog the blankets	15
Look much different without:	
Your teeth	127
Your hair	187
Your wedding ring	80
Have unconventional beauty:	
Face-lift	20
Tummy tuck	23
Implants	45

Installed by a taxidermist
(a bargain rate) 100

Bun tightening 30

Botox 21

Chemical peel 24

Eyes done 19

All of the above 78

Are a tad "different":

Formerly a man 155

Formerly a woman 166

Jury still out 541

SEXUAL CONDUCT

Ethics of sexually related weight loss: Is it ever proper to have sex with someone just for their body? Absolutely, especially if:

1. Such person is a hunk (a Club Med lifeguard or Hans, the stable boy, for instance).

2. Such person is a hunkess (a comely paralegal or a buxom congresswoman).

3. Such person speaks no English so you can't possibly know their mind.

4. Such person speaks English but she's a well-built floozy.

5. It's been nineteen months since your divorce, and you've had three cosmopolitans followed by two glasses of champagne.

6. Such person has been certified an official "Boy Toy" by NOW.

Statistic: 87% of all heterosexual couples approve of same-sex sex as long as they get to watch.

AROUSAL (ADVANCED): ORAL SEX

Not just a legitimate expression of your devotion, it's also a nice way to patch things up if you forgot to buy your partner a birthday gift. Be cautioned, however, that it burns immense quantities of calories—after only three hours of oral sex our test couple lost a combined 28 pounds and couldn't see over the steering wheel. Some weight loss figures from the National Pleasure Confederation:

ACTIVITY	CALORIES BURNED
Donning lobster bib	13
Doing it	44

If you're:	
Squeamish	66
Cursed with a super-keen gag reflex	1,639

Pausing for a second wind	9

Pausing for halvah	140
(Provides twice the energy of a granola bar.)	

If partner an expert	50
And has a handlebar mustache	299

Further information:

- Tartar control? Yes.

- Burns baby fat? Yes.

- Effective antiwrinkle restructuring night repair and firming action? Yes.

- Tones facial muscles? Yes (66% of participants report firmer skin and lovelier crow's feet).

- Can ease pre-exam jitters? Yes.

- Okay to practice on a pacifier if partner touring? Yes (Klondike Bar good too).

- Fun to do in a Mini Cooper? Yes, but watch for oncoming traffic.

REMOVING HAIR

AREA	CALORIES BURNED
From tongue	4

(A relatively simple operation involving thumb
and index finger. Be discreet and don't braid it.)

From roof of mouth	18

(Slightly more complicated. Finger, tip of tongue,
and pair of chopsticks may be necessary.)

From soft palate	114

(Very complicated, especially if it is sticking.
You may have to use tongue plus a couple
of your fingers, or, if it's stubborn, you may
have to borrow two of your partner's fingers.
Be persistent.)

From uvula	231

(One of the more volatile portions of the
anatomy. Hair twirled around the uvula is best
extracted with pliers, a vacuum cleaner, or by
rinsing with warm Snapple. Partner may notice.)

From throat 323
(Unless there's a small mop handy, just swallow
the hair. Only 2 calories per strand, 3 if it's
moussed.)

*Etiquette Tip: If you're getting desperate, it's
permissible to call a time-out.*

DISPOSING OF HAIR

Once you have successfully extracted the hair, you must dispose of it without offending your partner ("Love me, love my hair"). Jettisoning it over the side of the bed would seem logical, except that a strand is so light it will probably stick to your fingers. You'll end up shaking your hand violently and accomplishing nothing except destroying the mood and scaring the dog. Consider the following alternatives:

ACTIVITY	CALORIES BURNED
Surreptitiously wiping it on the sheet	1
Wiping it on partner	3
Putting it back where you found it	129

Fond Memories Suggestion: If it turns out to be your lover's first gray hair, frame it.

VII.
INTERCOURSE AND THINGS RELATED

Not just another weight loss gimmick, intercourse usually follows foreplay directly, except in the case of extremely spirited foreplay, in which case it might be wise to wait a day or two. Since intercourse puts such a severe strain on our physical and mental resources—it can burn up to 966 calories if partners are using bunk beds—we should be alert to the following warning signs of sexual enfeeblement:

1. Fatigue.

2. Inability to name the presidents in order.

3. Decreased interest in global warming.

4. Irregularity.

5. A morbid craving for flanken.

6. Loss of sensation below the hairline.

7. Collecting hip-hop videos.

8. Change of birth sign.

9. Persistent need for reassurance.

10. Sleeping in pajamas.

11. Watching C-SPAN.

Health Precaution: Unless you're in Switzerland, cease all sexual activity when partner begins to yodel.

DOING IT FOR THE FIRST TIME

Don't panic if the earth doesn't move.* The first time is usually more intellectual than physical. Many people, in fact, find themselves drawn to the word "fiasco" when called upon to describe their initial experience. "Catastrophe," "botch," "tragedy," and "lawsuit" are also sometimes used. Happily, most problems dissolve with time, patience, practice, and several glasses of an amusing Chablis. Indeed, it is not unusual for the sexually gifted to go from incompetence to greatness in just one weekend, providing your ex has the kids. Some first-time problems include:

ACTIVITY	CALORIES BURNED
Fumbling around	7

*Do panic if he doesn't move.

ACTIVITY	CALORIES BURNED

Desperately trying to put
something somewhere 18

    Missing 2

    Not realizing you missed 55

Embarrassment 158

Apologizing 91

Promising to try harder 16

    If partner is already:

        Asleep 20

        Gone 144

Remembering your first time if:

    It was good 21

    It was bad 33

    You had it bronzed 70

ACHIEVING ERECTION

ACTIVITY	CALORIES BURNED
For normal healthy man	2¼
For normal healthy woman	549
For normal healthy man whose partner has just said, "That's it?"	866

SUSTAINING ERECTION

Men who consider this a woman's responsibility just lie there with their fingers crossed, hoping something good will happen. One of our female dieters spent three hours trying to arouse an actor (he was reading for a part), during which time she lost three pounds but grew so weak that her life began to flash before her eyes.

ACTIVITY	CALORIES BURNED
For man	44
For woman	1,637

ERECTILE DIFFICULTIES

Most likely the problem is minor—she's using ice tongs, or he's just received a subpoena—and with an understanding partner, it will usually correct itself by January.

CAUSE	CALORIES BURNED
Pressure to perform .... 30 (Partner tapping it with a breadstick is considered pressure to perform.)	
Mildew 14	
Nerves:	
Fear of being inadequate 177	
Partner asking how many children he wants 841	
IRS disallowed tax shelter 50	
Senior moment .... 8 (Partner showing him photos of her grandchildren)	

Medication:

Zocor 32

Aunt Sadie's whitefish 40

Tainted Viagra 29
(Source: On-line Estonian pharmacy.)

Advisory: Until her partner recovers, the aroused woman can achieve satisfaction with Robbie, the Inflatable Bus Mechanic, sold at better boutiques.

WEIGHT LOSS BONUS #6: HIDE AND SEEK

ACTIVITY	CARB GRAMS BURNED
Losing erection	1½
Searching for it	115

PUTTING ON CONDOM

It is generally best to wait until you're ready. Men who try to save time by putting it on in advance—while pulling into the driveway, as they're flossing—are doomed to failure.

ACTIVITY	CALORIES BURNED
With erection	1¼
Without erection	300

Note: Myopic men too vain to wear their glasses should aim carefully. The possibility of inadvertently putting the condom on your foot is not remote.

INSERTING DIAPHRAGM

ACTIVITY	CALORIES BURNED
If woman who does it is:	
Experienced	6
Inexperienced	75
If man does it, regardless of experience	264
Chasing it across the room	600

DECIDING POSITION

Professional dieter-lovers tell us that any sexual position—from the popular missionary to the somewhat arcane but certainly pleasurable Goldberg Variation—is a good one, especially for lovers who are flexible enough to touch their toes without using a push broom. Lovers, however, who are indecisive—who agonize that no matter what position they choose a better one might come along—can avail themselves of the following methods:

ACTIVITY	CALORIES BURNED
Tossing a coin	4
Cutting cards	5
Arm wrestling	127
Age before beauty	10
(Works particularly well if he's eighty-seven, occupation: billionaire, and she's twenty-one, occupation: arm candy.)	
Ouija board	14

Calling trusted adviser:

Astrologer 11

Mom 142

Personal trainer 16
(Don't bother if your partner is your
personal trainer.)

Seniority 15

INSERTION: PART I

ACTIVITY	CALORIES BURNED
If man is ready .... ¼
If woman is not 274

> *Point of Sexual Etiquette: If he's had a difficult day, the caring female partner will help him climb on, giving him a little boost and using words of encouragement, such as "C'mon, Romeo, you can do it, just a little higher ... don't be a quitter." He'll be grateful.*

INSERTION: PART II

ACTIVITY	CALORIES BURNED
If woman is ready .... ½
If man is not 300*

*Inability to Cut the Mustard Advisory: If her partner fails to function, the truly secure woman continues without him.

SATISFYING HIS PARTNER

Experts agree: Size means nothing. Proportion is what counts—the man with an organ shaped like Sweden can name his price. In those rare instances where the male member is genuinely size-challenged (1.8 inches), he may have to compensate by working harder—an excellent way to achieve his weight loss goal. A man, on the other hand, who is well endowed,* while he may not have to work as hard, may exhaust himself just trying to convince his partner to let him proceed.

ACTIVITY	CALORIES BURNED
Normal, everyday size	22
Oversize	15
Magnifico	7
Teensy-weensy	170

*Two or more feet.

THE 1,001 POSITIONS OF LOVE

Out-of-shape dieters will gasp—
1,001 positions? With my back?
Not to worry. This figure is merely
the number of *possible* positions according
to (a) the pop-up Kama Sutra and (b) the
Office of Homeland Security. For our purposes we need discuss only those positions
that are easily executed, requiring neither
special agility nor bizarre erotic equip-
ment like a dentist's chair or winch.

ACTIVITY	CALORIES BURNED
Regular missionary 45	
The gold standard of positions. Not overly imaginative but enables both partners to self-ignite even if it's Lent. A favorite of couples trying to start (a) a family or (b) their heart.	
Irregular missionary (female partner on top, male partner on bottom) 51	
Preferred by women who either want to control their own orgasm or listen for the baby crying.	

Standing up (facing each other) 68
The hands-down favorite of partners suffering
hemorrhoidal flare-up. Works best if both
partners are of equal height. For differences
of one or more feet (homecoming queen with
a pixie, for instance), the shorter partner may
use stilts.

Standing up (back to back) 749
Usually employed by couples seeking to avoid a
love child. Also an option for ultraconservative
couples residing in the Bible Belt who maintain
that sex with a partner other than kin is a sin.

Park and ride 120
The preferred position for suburban couples
who commute.

WEIGHT LOSS BONUS #7: TWO ALTERNATIVE POSITIONS

ACTIVITY	CARB GRAMS BURNED
Man on top, woman suddenly realizing what was wrong with her first marriage	159
Lawyer on top, man under oath	377

INTERCOURSE: PART I

The ultimate way to explore each other's inner dieter, especially if you do it to reggae. A word of caution, however: Pace yourselves. Begin too slowly and your partner loses interest. Begin too fast and you get chest pains. The approved stages (your mileage may vary):

ACTIVITY	CALORIES BURNED
Starting	3
Moderate (on cruise control)	15
Picking up the pace	19
Doing the salsa	64
Enthusiastic wheezing	68
Shifting into high gear	135
Wild abandon	255
Muttering, "Are you close?"	42
Spirited pounding	388
Incoherent convulsions	446
Demonic possession	579

Point of Sexual Etiquette: It is the partner who's done the least work who gets out of bed to provide the warm washcloth.

INTERCOURSE: PART II

ACTIVITY	CALORIES BURNED
If he takes his time 300	
If he's just like all the others 11	

THINGS OFTEN SAID DURING SEX

ACTIVITY	CALORIES BURNED
"Leave the lights on, I have to watch my cholesterol."	5
"Ssshhh, we'll wake:	
. . . the kids."	9
. . . your mother."	44
"Goodness, where'd you learn *that*?"	12
"You want me to do *what*?"	10
"Faster!"	5
"You call that faster?"	9
"Harder!"	3
"Too hard!"	11
"Too soft!"	9
"Do you think there's any film in that news camera?"	16
"It's all in the wrist."	12
"I'm soooooooooooooooo close."	18
"Leg cramp! Leg cramp!"	25
"My heart, my heart!"	66

ACTIVITY	CALORIES BURNED
"Missed you at Bible study."	10
"Maybe we ought to get married again?"	17
"When I moan, can you tell I had garlic?"	5
"Let me get on top—your pearls are hitting my teeth."	29
"You're smudging our eye shadow." (same sex marriages only)	13
I wish our workstation were bigger."	16

SILENCE IS SEXY

Though it consumes fewer calories, in-bed nonverbal communication—a brief stroke, a gentle caress, or cash—between understanding partners can be more effective than words.

ACTIVITY	CALORIES BURNED
Pointing to what you want . . . . 8 (For best results, use the same motion as when standing before a buffet table.)	
Tugging on what you want:	
For tugger 3	
For tuggee 144	

Financial Tip: Quiet the lover who makes too much noise during sex with hush money.

MIXED MESSAGES: A PRIMER FOR THE INEXPERIENCED MALE

WHAT SHE SAYS	WHAT SHE'S THINKING
"Let's try something different."	My leg is falling asleep.
"Yes, yes, yes, yes, yes, yes."	Yes.
"I didn't know you could last so long."	Snap it up. We have ballet tickets.
"Are you sure you'll respect me in the morning?"	I may need you to do some chores.
"I never felt this way before."	. . . in this particular city.
"I didn't know it could be this good."	But can he hang a door?
"I'll try anything."	Except that.

WHAT SHE SAYS	WHAT SHE'S THINKING
"I'm your slave."	Would this guy freak if I asked to be spanked?
"We're falling off the bed."	We're falling off the bed.
"I could lie here forever."	I'd kill for an Oreo.

CHANGING POSITIONS

Frequently switching positions keeps sex fresh and interesting and, for partners with delicate skin, prevents chafing. For best results, the change should be effected in one fluid motion—a gentle U-turn rather than a K-turn or, more injurious to the ego, saying, "Get off me"— being careful not to (a) break the rhythm or (b) send yourselves into the next zip code.

ACTIVITY	CALORIES BURNED
Stopping	3
Without stopping	58

Changing positions is advised if:

• You find yourselves sliding off the bed. (Satin sheets? Prevent skidding by wearing deck shoes.)

- You've moved up too far—one partner's head is repeatedly slamming into the headboard, making it difficult to concentrate and, if it's New Year's Eve, keep your party hat on.
- Mood swing is imminent.
- It's step twelve of your Twelve-Step Program.
- You're getting out of camera range.

KEEPING SEX EXCITING

A bed is good, but spontaneity is the cornerstone of a happy sex life, as long as you don't block a fire exit. Adventurous lovers, limited only by their imagination and their upbringing, can make their fantasies come true while burning calories.

ACTIVITY	CALORIES BURNED
Hot tub skinny dipping	159
Kids away on a sleepover	893
For those who love adventure:	
Lonely farmhouse	65
Dorm stairwell	79
While going through a car wash	50
(Moving violation in West Virginia.)	
In a hammock	75
On the White House lawn	1,682

Scenic overlook at sunset:

Dressing room:

Mile High Club:

Outdoor Sex Tip: Partner wearing the backpack should be on top.

Lovers Without Borders: Once a month make love someplace where you have to show a passport—like Paris, or a rice paddy.

ARE WE DOING IT CORRECTLY?

An appropriate question for novice lovers, as well as the newly divorced whose personal ads are starting to bear fruit. Experienced lovers rely on their "sexual radar" to determine if all's going well: Are her eyes sparkling? Is he letting his knish get cold? Have you both lost interest in multiculturalism? Some guidelines:

1. Strange noises. A good thing. In the latter stages of ecstasy (Stage VIII), it is not unusual for the female, when biting her partner's arm, to either squeal or, if she's petite, chirp. Similarly, the male partner, as he approaches the "final moment," may start counting backwards from ten or, if he can't find his fingers in the dark, simply moan in Latin or, more authentically, in Aramaic.

2. A partner repeating the phrase, "Don't stop, don't stop," thirty or more times a minute indicates you are on the right

track. Apply a cold compress to your partner's head should he begin to ferment.

3. Sex that lasts fifty or more minutes can precipitate dehydration and a protein deficiency. We suggest water and lox.

4. Panting. A partner-response alert indicating that your ear nibbles are working. Environment-conscious lovers will be happy to note that vigorous panting actually repairs the ozone layer.

5. Writhing. A serpentine movement that, if partner is sufficiently aroused, can burn up to 50 calories per writhe. (Note: Zero calories burned if writhing caused by boredom.)

6. Blushing. Extra calories are burned if partner blushes in primary colors such as an honest red or a bold violet. (A washed-out pink or a tepid magenta consumes, at best, 2 calories.)

7. Premature ejaculation. Not a problem so long as it doesn't occur while he's mixing the salad. It's called "immature ejaculation" if partner fears commitment.

Note: You are doing it correctly if your leg falls asleep before he does.

HOW OFTEN SHOULD WE DO IT?

There is no pat answer. The government's Pleasure Czar suggests a frequency rate ranging from thirty-six times a week for newlyweds to once a month for those living near a golf course. For lovers who like to "keep up with the Joneses," we offer the more precise figures below, prepared by our steering committee and based on the national average.

IF YOU ARE	USUAL FREQUENCY RATE	UNUSUAL FREQUENCY RATE
A typical couple	Once weekly	Daily, either twice in the morning or twice at bedtime
A typical couple and the kids have left for college	Twice weekly or eight times on last day of the month	Once monthly if in-laws moved into spare room

A decadent couple	15 times weekly	24 times weekly if you have trouble sleeping
New parents	Never	Once on Mother's Day
On your first honeymoon	3 times daily	5 times daily (if it rains)
On second honeymoon	Once daily	1½ times daily
Married 12 to 20 years	3 times weekly	5 times weakly
A dual-career couple	12 times yearly	About the same
A dual-career couple with conflicting hours	Once every other Valentine's Day	Once every Valentine's Day
Both in a nursing home	Once	As needed
Bridge fanatics	Once	As needed

WEIGHT LOSS BONUS #8: ANXIETY

ACTIVITY	CARB GRAMS BURNED
Condom broke 57
Water broke 294

APPROACHING ORGASM

While surrendering to the moment is admirable, teetering on the brink burns more calories. Lovers who, despite the intensity of feeling, lie there calmly, perhaps blowing bubbles on a bubble pipe, can burn far more calories and emerge from the experience significantly thinner.

ACTIVITY	CALORIES BURNED
Really letting yourself go	4
Controlling yourself (may require a little pep talk):	
So partner won't think you're not a lady	58
Because in-laws in the next room	76
(Easy to do: Simply gnaw on an unused corner of the pillowcase.)	

ACTIVITY	CALORIES BURNED

Digging nails into:

    Partner's back 11

    Your back 165

Things escalating 33
(You can tell—you're chewing your gum
faster, much faster.)

Trembling 15

Shaking 17

Shuddering 19

Trying to keep eyes open:

    So you can see your lover's face 23

    So you can see the time 50

VIII. ORGASM, AND BEYOND

I told him that during orgasm, if I lose control, grab the sheets, bite my knuckles, call out the name of my furrier, writhe, moan, and shout, "More peanut brittle!" it means I'm having fun, and to please not call security.*

—TRISH GARDENIA, STARLET, REALITY SHOW

Contrary to the advice of weight loss experts, the most calories are not burned by during-climax facial expressions. It's the little things that count. We found, for instance, that orgasmic calories are doubled for the woman wearing a lab coat. And the truly sensitive male can easily triple carb grams burned if his partner is showing vacation slides. What every serious dieter should know about orgasm:

*Based on a true story.

- It's surprisingly affordable.
- It burns calories and fat grams simultaneously!
- You can't have too many.
- You can have too few. (One every Valentine's Day is too few.)
- A real one can't be faked.
- It wards off evil spirits, even if they bring a house gift.
- The ability to have them is a natural skill.
- The ability to give them is a marketable skill.

WEIGHT LOSS BONUS #9: GETTING CLOSER

The transition from approaching orgasm to being just a few seconds away should occur naturally, without stopping to ask your partner, "What's your favorite color?" or make a difficult career decision. Additional things never to do as you near climax . . . unless you're desperate to lose extra weight:

ACTIVITY	CARB GRAMS BURNED
Wave at a passing neighbor	5
Practice the harmonica	7
Lean over to:	
Better sniff the incense	4
Read an incoming fax	11
Apply more antiperspirant	2
Call a radio therapist for advice	7
Sort laundry	15

CHIVALRY
AND DIETING

Traditionally, the male partner, ever gallant and concerned with his partner's pleasure, *always* delays his orgasm until either she has hers, or his pelvis shatters.* Unfortunately certain women, due, perhaps, to sudden recollection of their vow of chastity or to the fact that they are doing two things at once (attempting climax while denouncing our foreign policy), may take up to seventy-eight minutes to climax, necessitating heroic efforts by her partner to (1) not climax first and (2) remember why he's there. Asking her, "What's taking you so long?" is not an option. Instead:

To Delay Climax For	Think About
5 minutes	Baseball (cricket for British lovers)

*Untraditionally, the male partner climaxes within four minutes, rolls over, and either falls asleep or asks if there's more ravioli.

10 minutes	Waiting on line at the post office
15 minutes	Achieving world peace (or, if you've already done that, solving world hunger)
20 minutes	That unopened notice from the IRS (please let it be just a thank-you note)
25 minutes	The recipe for a perfect braised lamb shank
30 minutes	How you like your steak cooked
35 minutes	PBS pledge week
40 minutes	Why one should never fertilize perennials
45 minutes	Early tee time
1 hour	Weather forecasters
Longer than 1 hour	Maybe it's me?

Advisory: Did She Really Achieve Satisfaction? Here's an easy way to tell: 92 percent of all women, at the moment of orgasm, either put down their iPod or lose their place in the novel they're reading.

ORGASM

ACTIVITY	CALORIES BURNED
Real	46
Faked	220
A little of both	133

Reality Check: Determine the intensity of partner's orgasmic pleasure by using a meat thermometer.

Nutrition Tip: Orgasm is nature's way of telling you to get up and make breakfast.

FAKING ORGASM

Why do some men "fake it"? Many reasons: Perhaps he's tired or he's taking strong medication, or an acting class. The extra-sensitive man may want to impress you with his staying power or have depression issues, especially if his car was dinged at the mall.

ACTIVITY	CALORIES BURNED
For him 10	
Convincingly 382	
(Caution: May cause sudden change of inseam.)	

GUILT: PART I

Whether you faked orgasm for the wrong reasons (wanted to see if you could do it convincingly) or the right reasons (the only way to get him to leave), confession is good for the soul—and body.

ACTIVITY	CALORIES BURNED
Confessing you faked it:	
To your nonjudgmental best friend	5
To your gynecologist	79
To your therapist:	
Strict Freudian	14
Strict hairdresser	137
To your clergyperson	50
Who shouts, "Let's go to the videotape!"	88
Who comes on to you	120
To your partner	100
On your Web site	22
On *Oprah*	250

ORGASMIC INTENSITY SCALE

The National Pleasure Alliance asked our experts for a quality rating of the orgasms most often experienced by dieters when they "pull out all the stops." Ratings are based on a minimum of five minutes of vigorous sex with a partner with a strong work ethic and who, when things heat up, snaps his fingers to Motown. The highest was 100 (sudden sinus relief) and the lowest was 2 (partner put her book down). Note: Quality of orgasm is more important than quantity, although one woman who experienced twenty-two so-so orgasms within a four-hour period swore her cheeks got rosier.

How long should an orgasm last? If you have lots of time, hours. If you have a customer waiting, seconds.

STRENGTH OF ORGASM	CALORIES BURNED
Toes clenched	9
Shoes flew off	28
Subdued tingling	5
Orchestra swelled	34
Heavenly choir sang	144
Finally passed that kidney stone	190
Birds sang:	
One large bird	17
A few small ones	14
Magical explosions	30
Roman candles	50
Blazing pinwheels	67
Vesuvius erupted	75
Trumpets blared	48
Earth moved	686
Mascara ran	99

Note: Dieters expecting immediate, even miraculous clearing of the complexion will be disappointed. There is only so much an orgasm can do.

WEIGHT LOSS BONUS #10: WILLPOWER

ACTIVITY	CARB GRAMS BURNED
Withdrawal:	
Moments after orgasm 1½	
Moments before orgasm 574	
(Useful as a form of birth control or if the	
Welcome Wagon suddenly shows up.)	

MULTIPLE ORGASMS FOR THE FEMALE PARTNER*

Depending on greed—and her rate of recovery—a woman can enjoy up to eight orgasms before revealing her PIN number and losing consciousness. As the number increases, however, she may begin to experience a form of "reduced sanity" that will temporarily interfere with her ability to cook, drive a minivan, and appreciate scat singing.

ORGASMS	CALORIES BURNED
Two	28
Five	139
Seven	252
Losing count	1,166

*Studies show that as she gets older, the multiorgasmic woman who really enjoys sex almost never turns into her mother.

MULTIPLE ORGASMS FOR THE MALE PARTNER

For a man, it's a different situation, due perhaps to physiological and biological reasons, or to eating free-range egg whites. Many men can enjoy up to four orgasms in an hour with little discomfort so long as they have their health and wear a Harley-Davidson jacket. With few exceptions, however, the man who tries to achieve more than ten orgasms within that same period sustains irreversible brain damage and has to go to work for the DMV.

ORGASMS	CALORIES BURNED
Two	70
Three	168
Four	300
Twelve (within a 60-minute period)	?*

*Though enthusiastic, subject suddenly turned inside out and lapsed into coma. He awoke several days later in Newark, New Jersey.

PREMATURE EJACULATION

A frequent result of the extreme anticipation experienced by a highly aroused male who is smitten with his partner's beauty. In rare instances, it may occur as he savors a thirty-year-old glass of port while puffing on a Cuban cigar.

TYPE OF ORGASM	CALORIES BURNED
During insertion 7	
During intercourse . . . . 11 (Officially "premature" if it occurs 1.4 seconds after insertion. A thoughtful male apologizes profusely, swears it will never happen again, and buys his partner a nice piece of jewelry.)	
During foreplay 15	
While parking the car 40	
Mature ejaculation . . . . 4 (A favorite of retirees and heads of state.)	

ACHIEVING ORGASM UNDER UNUSUAL CIRCUMSTANCES

TYPE OF ORGASM	**CALORIES BURNED**
While donating blood	19
While threading a needle	22
While donating an organ:	
Kidney	200
Wurlitzer	33
After two bottles of wine	47
While holding for the next customer service representative	30
While talking on the phone*	5
In the mattress section at Sears	54
If you're honeymooners and the airline lost:	
Your luggage	27
Your diaphragm	70
While negotiating a car loan	41

*Movie producers have this down to a science.

TYPE OF ORGASM	CALORIES BURNED
While donating sperm:	
Alone	49
With helper	2

SPECIAL ORGASMS

TYPE OF ORGASM	CALORIES BURNED
Clitoral	41
Vaginal	85
Both at same time	377
Time release	155
Can't recall your Social Security number	61
While applying eyeliner	80
Making last mortgage payment	100

AFTER SEX

IX. AFTERPLAY

What happens directly after sex is just as important as what happened during. Some people immediately light a cigarette. Others put one out. The caring woman asks her partner, "Do you need help getting off me?" Dieting lovers concentrate on making their partner feel that it was totally satisfying and wonderful, instead of glancing at their watch, rushing into the bathroom, and trying to remember where they left their car keys.

In this section you will learn of the benefits of not instantly falling asleep, which burns a mere 2 carb grams and could make your partner do something hostile, like sneak out of bed and withdraw all your money from an ATM. The recovery table below, prepared by the Conservative Institute of Erotic Studies, will interest those affected with Post-Lovemaking Stress Syndrome, a sign of which will be a partner's valiant but unsuccessful effort to explain Dark Matter.

AFTER SEX, A LOVER SHOULD BE ABLE TO	IN
Roll over and fall asleep	2 seconds
Grant an encore:	
To him	5 minutes
To her	4 hours
Operate heavy machinery:	
Tractor	1 hour
Cell phone	1 minute
TV remote	5 seconds
(Or 3 seconds if World Series on.)	
Accessorize a new spring wardrobe	2–3 hours
Check the clock to see where the time went	1 minute
Check the scale to see where the weight went	2 minutes

WEIGHT LOSS BONUS #11: THE WET SPOT

ACTIVITY	CARB GRAMS BURNED
Avoiding the wet spot 20	

Point of Sexual Etiquette: Feminists may quibble, but unless the wet spot is moisturizer-related, chivalry dictates that the male partner lie in any wet spot caused by:

- *Him*
- *Flop sweat*
- *The tide*
- *Fire sprinklers*

MID-DIET PROGRESS REPORT

1. How are things going?
   □ Great, just like you said they would.
   □ Not bad, but so much sex, so little time.

2. Pounds lost: ___.

3. Pounds to go: ___.

4. I burned the most calories during:
   □ Intense foreplay.
   □ Feverish intercourse.
   □ Fervent begging.

5. I plan to lose more weight by:
   □ Continuing to have sex.
   □ Finding a new partner (think I'm
      wearing my current one out).
   □ Retraining the partner I already have.

6. My partner still considers me a person of
   mystery.
   □ False.
   □ Only when I wear lots of makeup.

7. I still believe sex is the most fun you can have:
   □ Without your clothes on.
   □ Without using a knife and fork.
   □ Without owning beachfront property.

8. Most productive surface on which to make love:
   □ The bed.
   □ The sofa.
   □ The bathroom scale.

9. This diet has made my lover and me:
   □ Closer.
   □ Thinner.
   □ Competitive.
   □ Appreciate fitted sheets.

10. Once we reach our desirable body weights we plan to maintain our new and wonderful figures by:
    □ Continuing to have lots of sex.
    □ Liposuction.
    □ Bulimia.

THINGS OFTEN SAID AFTER SEX*

After-sex utterances can range from the complimentary ("Who'd have thought you were a screamer?") to the diplomatic ("I'd stay over, but my plants will wonder where I am"), and although they're considered low-weight-loss activities, we firmly believe that every little calorie helps.

TYPICAL UTTERANCES	CALORIES BURNED
"How cool was that?"	8
"Thanks for not waking me."	11
"Wow, I never did that with my ex."	10
"I think I pulled something."	3
"Thank you, it's been so long."	20
"Are you seeing anyone else?"	17
"Can you tell I didn't fake it?"	9
"Was it good for you?"	5
"Was it good for me?"	12

*For partners with zero pleasure tolerance, "Whew, it's finally over" is not a recognized calorie burner.

TYPICAL UTTERANCES	CALORIES BURNED
"Have you seen my wedding band?"	7
"I couldn't have done it without you."	14
"You just lie there, sweetie, I'll handle the merger."	21
"Don't take this the wrong way, but you're lousy in bed."	75
And let us not forget those after-sex words of magic: "We're thinner!"	30

THING OFTEN
DONE AFTER SEX

ACTIVITY	CALORIES BURNED
Spooning	25

THING OFTEN
THOUGHT AFTER
A NIGHT OF
INCREDIBLE SEX

ACTIVITY	CALORIES BURNED
Can I get away with wearing the same outfit to work?	69

17 THINGS TO BE HAPPY ABOUT AFTER SEX

As you blink away tears of joy, here are the passion-related rewards, other than weight loss and the sudden disappearance of liver spots, for dieters to rejoice over:

1. He's staying the night (doesn't count if it's his apartment).

2. You discovered a new position.

3. The old one worked nicely, too.

4. You're blushing.

5. Your urologist was wrong.

6. So was your horoscope.

7. She wanted you for your body *and* your mind.

8. Lower cholesterol.

9. Higher cheekbones.

10. Your ex took the kids.

11. Your mother called . . . the answering machine was on mute.

12. The baby kept its promise not to cry.

13. Your guests downstairs were patient.

14. Acne? Gone.

15. Cuddling.

16. Your lover also cooks.

17. She promised to call.

POSSIBLE SIDE EFFECTS OF GOOD SEX

Instant promotion to your partner's A-list —your photo as partner's screensaver, for instance—is usually the first indication that sex was a positive experience. You may also feel light, as though you were dozing in a vat of cream cheese. If sex was really terrific, you'll feel dangerously—but pleasantly—drained, as if your body had been connected to a high-tech milking machine, and you might have to be stabilized with tea and toast. Additional reactions include:

ACTIVITY	CALORIES BURNED
Afterglow	14
Totally at peace with the world	10
A sunny disposition	22
Grinning in your work cubicle	9

ROLLING OVER AND GOING TO SLEEP

ACTIVITY	CALORIES BURNED

Moments after intercourse 18
Classic behavior for certain men who believe
they've "done their job" and are now entitled to
sleep. The wise dieter, however, knowing that
his partner wants to talk and be held, stays
awake for at least five minutes and, by doing
so, burns an extra 40 calories!

During intercourse 32

If partner couldn't tell 70

ACTIVITY	CALORIES BURNED

During foreplay 20
Indicates either a serious lack of interest or
advanced fatigue. The partner still awake should
continue as though everything's fine. (Need a
substitute partner? Use a tailor's dummy.)

During a dinner party 7
(Situation hopeless.)

*Morning Sex Tip: Newton's tenth, and possibly
least understood, law of gravity holds that the
more snuggly your partner, the more difficult it
will be, especially on a cold winter morning, to
get out of a nice warm bed, especially if you
have to go to work. The five stages of post-
snooze-alarm unentwining include:*

ACTIVITY	*CALORIES BURNED*

"It's time to get up." 2

"We'd better get up." 3

"It's really getting late." 5

"My God, look at the time!" 9

"Let's call in sick." 1

10 TOP REASONS LOVERS ROLL OVER AND GO TO SLEEP

Fortunately for dieters, sleep is not as passive an activity as one might imagine. It has, in fact, more calorie-burning potential* than many waking-hour activities. Confirmed late sleepers will find, to their delight, that the agony of getting up at 6:30 A.M. on a cold, rainy morning and hopping on their moped to report to their post at Kmart is calorically equivalent to three hours of karaoke in front of a peace rally. (It should also be noted that the speed at which one sleeps greatly influences calories consumed.) Calorie counts reflect effort required to fall into a deep, sound sleep.

*Especially during that magical period between sleepy and asleep, a state known as "sleepish."

REASON	CALORIES BURNED
Heredity	22
Habit	14
Tried the 166 positions listed in the *Arabian Book of Eagerness*	166
Too much of that arrogant little Syrah	2
Laziness	5
Aversion to after-sex small talk	7
Partner a dream to burrow under the covers with	½
Late shift	6
Nothing better to do	8
Partner practicing speech to local chamber of commerce	¼

SLEEP

ACTIVITY	CALORIES BURNED
Real 5
Faked 74

A good way to avoid a sex-crazed partner who
won't give up. This can happen if you go to bed
with someone just for sex, which is a sin.
Wearing a sleeping mask may or may not
convince your partner that you're not faking.
We make no guarantees.

TRYING AGAIN

ACTIVITY	CALORIES BURNED
If she is ready 3
If he is not 475

THANKING PARTNER FOR A WONDERFUL NIGHT

The problem with quickie sex is that the cars behind us start honking the moment the light changes. —IVANA, TV PERSONALITY

Shun prepackaged sentiment—cards, stuffed bears, a cashier's check—and express your own feelings.* If you have writer's block, stimulate the creative juices by pressing the bedsheets to your bosom. (Dieters take note: Pressing the entire bed to your bosom burns more calories.) And, unless you're calligraphically challenged, your billet-doux should be handwritten (pencils with spell check available at most upscale stationers).

*SAMPLE ONLY: "My Dearest Pumpkin: As I sit here on my lonely bed, the world is a cold, cold place without your warmth, your radiant smile . . ."

Sending an intimate note:

By mail 9
(Enclose a lock of your hair.)

By messenger:

FedEx 14

Carrier pigeon 20
(Rated A for Romance by the National
Bird Society.)

Sending a singing telegram:

You 155

A pro:

Out-of-work singer 25

Bob Dylan 690

*Tip: You can really show how wonderful the
night was by giving your lover more closet
space.*

MAKING THE BED

ACTIVITY	CALORIES BURNED
With partner still in it 44
With you still in it 197

AFTER SEX AMAZING *AND* EXTRAORDINARY?

ur favorite quick-weight-loss after-sex calorie burners:

1. Giving thanks.

2. Uncrossing eyes.

3. Sweeping crumbs off sheet (if you ordered in).

4. Calling best friend.

5. Righting the night stand.

6. Removing candle wax.

7. Straightening the pictures.

8. De-wilting the plants.

9. Finding that other earring.

10. Regaining composure.

11. Regaining reputation.

12. Six-hour nap.

13. Dressing each other (a nice courtesy).

14. Rolling down the windows if you've just gone through a car wash.

15. Producing a male heir.

16. Dreaming about the next time.

17. Eating leftovers.

SHOULD YOU INVITE YOUR PARTNER BACK?

Although a factor, quality of sex should not unduly influence your decision. Ask yourself the following questions:

1. Is this the person I want someday to carve a jack-o'-lantern with?

2. Did I have to fake sleep to get this person to leave?

3. Did he make me wait in the hall while he called his ex?

4. After he left was there anything missing—towels, sheets, silverware?

5. Inventory medicine cabinet. Everything exactly the way I left it? (If necessary, dust for fingerprints.)

6. Drinking problem? Was there a flask of gin in her coat pocket? Did she offer to share?

7. Willpower problem? During sex did he sneak into the bathroom for a cigarette? Twice?

8. Which CDs put partner in romantic mood?
   □ Beethoven piano trios
   □ Perry Como
   □ *Chicks on Speed*
   □ *Bjork on Speed*
   □ *The Cole Porter Songbook*
   □ Our national anthem

9. Will my parents approve?

10. Does my cat approve?

11. Were the wet panty hose in his gym bag his?

Note: All is forgiven for the partner who, within three minutes of the commencement of sex, goes where no one ever went before: your G spot.

FAILURE TO CALL AFTER A NIGHT OF INCREDIBLE LUST

Several brokenhearted dieters asked that we include a section on why it is wrong (and possibly unethical if he did your laundry) for a new partner, after sex, to renege on their promise to call. The mental picture of a sobbing dieter, sitting by the phone in his underwear, waiting for her to call and realizing, after seven months, that he was a "one-night stand" induced us to set forth the following precepts. (Note: They apply to women only. The male dieter-lover is a gentleman and always calls if he says he will.)

1. Do not promise to call just to get out of there graciously—it only gets his hopes up. "I'm off to the convent" or "I joined the Peace Corps, they're sending me to Trump Tower" is less devastating.

2. Calling just to ask, "Did I leave my watch/
earring/cell phone charger/leftover wedge
of brie there?" and asking him to messenger
it over suggests you're not eager for personal
contact. Again, ruinous to his ego. Instead,
wait until he's not home and break in.

3. If he loses his cool, calls you twenty or more
times, and keeps getting your machine, he
will, unless he's the Terminator, get the
message.* He will also get a powerful I-
need-my-space message if you take his call
and put him on hold for three weeks, but
that's also cowardly.

4. Unless you're one of those goody two-
shoes, a teeny white lie—you're going
back to your:
   □ husband
   □ boyfriend
   □ roots
   □ platoon
   —is evil only if you're caught.

5. If the sex was really good, he'll probably,
as you're leaving, offer gas money. Take it.

*"If this is Jason with the bad teeth, hang up immediately" worked
nicely for one woman.

METROSEXUAL AFTER-SEX JITTERS

TYPICAL POSTLOVEMAKING TRAUMAS OFTEN EXPERIENCED BY THE METROSEXUAL

(Note: Each trauma burns approximately 120 calories. The bonus trauma burns 2,866 calories.)

1. Couldn't find other sock.

2. Had sex on nondesigner sheets.

3. Wearing a fresh flower behind my ear didn't excite her (but she loved my buttermilk-raspberry waffles).

4. Forgot to manscape (a form of topiary in which the chest hair is carefully shaved, ideally in the form of a crop circle).

5. Tears of ecstasy made my mascara run.

6. Her love bites ruined my tan.

7. She served our after-lovemaking champagne in juice glasses. Hel-lo!

8. Battered cuticle.

9. New spider vein.

10. Couldn't find my Aqua Net.

Bonus Trauma: I feel so used.

> *Note: Experts suggest a causal connection between metrosexuality and having been circumcised with pinking shears.*

X. SUPPLE-
MENTARY
PLEASURES
AND
DELIGHTS

S o much activity is compressed into sex that we often fail to realize that weight loss never stops. Did you know, for instance, that erotic fantasy can burn an additional 20 calories, even more if it involves either (a) a threesome or (b) unlimited entrée to Disney World? Or that a depraved bondage-discipline session (see *Spanking Masters of the Senate, Part V: Thigh-High Stilettos*) may actually reduce your waistline? In this section we will see how the so-called fringe areas of sex—crying yourself to sleep, supplementing orgasm with little booster rockets, introducing a new line of sportswear, and so on—can play an important role not just in weight loss, but in making sex extra special.

Note: If you have a spare moment, this is the time to search for any as yet undiscovered G spots. You'll know you found another one if your grateful partner:
1. Moans and kicks the covers off the bed.
2. Offers to cosign your loan.

FANTASIES

Fantasy enables couples to exercise their imaginations and explore the naughty side of sex without (a) tainting themselves or (b) going to jail. Their fantasies come true if (a) they're adventurous and (b) they've purchased sufficient lubricant. Some common sexual fantasies and the calories burned while thinking about them:

ACTIVITY	CALORIES BURNED
Six fantasies for him:	
1. Sex slave to five insomniac starlets	90
2. Erotic bubble bath with a Quaker wearing only a wool cap	25
3. Love wrestling with an eggplant (no penetration)	30
4. Massaging Jimmy Choos (and licking the shoe box)	17
5. Deflowering an elf who is wearing a tiny rubber raincoat	15
6. Running 4 miles in the galoshes of my beloved	48

Six fantasies for her:

FANTASIES FOR BOTH

1. Oriental-medical theme. My partner is beating me with a chopstick. Flakes of General Tso's chicken fly about the room. The pleasure is unspeakable. I cry out for more. She switches to Lake Tung-Ting shrimp and uses a tongue depressor. Much better. Our moans of pleasure wake my mother-in-law. She runs from the house and is never heard from again.

2. Might makes right. My partner and I are law enforcement officers. We respond to a 911 call from the Neighborhood Watch and burst into a bedroom where two individuals are engaged in same-sex sex. They let us watch. Afterward, they cook an amazing prosciutto and mushroom frittata for four served with two bottles of Chardonnay, Grammy Pushkin's soda bread, and raspberry mousse for dessert. We then cuff them and take them to jail.

3. The great outdoors. I am in our garden, selecting the perfect herbs for tonight's

gefilte fish. Yakov, the coarse pig farmer from the cottage next door, sneaks up behind me, lifts my Prada tie-dyed stretch poplin fringed miniskirt, and takes me. I feel his hot breath on my neck. He whispers words of love in my ear, "Ahhdggg," "Oy oy oy oy," and "Hoo ha." Afterward, he whispers, "This is for you," and gives me a pork loin.

4. Food. I am naked except for a pair of leather gloves and my toe ring. My partner is dressed as Batman. He covers my body with fresh-baked, still-warm chocolate chip cookies and gives me a pedicure with his teeth. He then eats his way north, taking the scenic route and lingering in several good places. I pass the time until he's finished by building a Lego fortress.

MASTURBATION: POSITION PAPER

Seed spillers we're not, but there are times and situations when sex between two consenting hands is appropriate, namely:

- Appearance on a reality show.
- Exercise.
- Tension relief (one Surgeon General, now deposed, insisted it could significantly boost one's grade point average).
- Pleasantly passing the time while waiting for a Domino's delivery.
- Pleasantly passing the time if you're serving a life sentence.
- Birth control.
- Warm-up.
- A surprisingly affordable way to keep warm.
- Anything for a laugh.
- Keeping your wrist from falling asleep.
- Celebrity sperm donor.

- Determining if the elastic in your elastic-waist pants is really that elastic.
- While waiting to tee off.
- It's steps 9 through 13 in reputable sexual addiction programs.

A DIETING LOVER'S DREAMLAND

ACTIVITY	CALORIES BURNED
Wet dreams (erotic)	22
Wet dreams (really erotic):	
Rapturous pineapple pizza	90
Flawless latkes	17
Voluptuous cheesecake	48
Superb spaghetti carbonara	37
French vanilla ice cream	60
Ecstatic barbecued ribs	65
Glorious meat loaf	56
Sultry sausage and pepper hero	70
Intoxicating fried chicken	51
Ardent chili	66
Seductive cherry danish	50
Densely intense chocolate cream pie . .	1,000

Health Advisory: An enormous dream that includes everything above can cause either death or a headache.

FETISHES

There is nothing abnormal about complementing one's sexual activities with common household items. Certain people, for instance, can achieve sexual gratification only when clutching a brick or fondling potatoes. Others derive pleasure from canaries with shaved heads. And there are those who prefer sex with sailors wearing wax lips. An erotic devotion to items such as leather, iron, cookie dough, and green nylon wigs merely suggests a lover who thinks for himself, rather than following others. We do not judge. For additional weight loss, sample one of the popular fetishes below:

ACTIVITY	CALORIES BURNED
Sex with any partner wearing a Peter Pan costume	45
Sex on a forklift	289
Any freshwater fish fetish	30

ACTIVITY	CALORIES BURNED

Insisting that partner, during
climax, call you Zeke 11

Sex in a frog outfit 58

Sex with a large layer cake 49

Cross-dressing:

    Iron cross 14

    Maltese cross 17

    Blue Cross 31

Caressing intimate apparel:

    Her daring plunge-front underwire
    demi-bra in poinsettia red with
    matching stretch-lace thong 28

    His bowling shirt 13

BONDAGE

Along with enhancing the sexual experience, bondage can also prevent a partner from (a) eating all the food and (b) leaving. A reliable bondage device can be anything from panty hose or leash to ultra-sophisticated restraint systems such as Poligrip and Twizzlers.

ACTIVITY	CALORIES BURNED
Binding partner with rope:	

The following knots have been approved by the Geneva Convention:

Sheepshank	7
Slipknot	8
Half hitch	9
Figure eight	11
Square knot	12

Binding partner with necktie:	
Windsor knot	9
Half Windsor	4½

For the knot-challenged we suggest:

Handcuffs	3
Shackles	6
Floss	27
Glue	10
Just ordering partner to "Stay!"	6

FAVORITE GAMES OF LIBERATED DIETERS

1. Harsh Heidi Paddles Naughty Washington Lobbyist

2. Mistress Mabel, the Asphyxiator of Tulsa

3. Take-No-Prisoners Scrabble

4. Bind Me, Gag Me, But Don't Forget to Feed Me

5. Reverse the Vasectomy™

6. Dentist

DISCIPLINE: S&M

A particular favorite of men who wear suits—lawyers, politicians, and weathermen. The more convincingly your partner begs you to stop, the more calories burned.

ACTIVITY	CALORIES BURNED
S	67
&	3
M	55
Thrashing partner with:	
Popsicle stick	2
Toothpick	½
Bootlace	4
(Add 22 calories if still in boot.)	
Sturdy length of licorice	7
Chicken wing	10
(Burns 10 extra calories if still attached to chicken.)	
Kosher salami	18
Pin	1

ACTIVITY	CALORIES BURNED
Close-order drill	32
By a Special Forces dominatrix	279

Note: Making partner write, five hundred times, "I will not chew gum during sex" is a form of discipline.

MAKING WHIPPIE

A ccording to resident whip expert Lew Marmelstein, whipping a willing partner with skill can aid greatly in spot reducing. The whipper should concentrate on particularly stubborn areas of the body—love handles, saddlebags, and those gross Milky Way-induced folds of skin at the bottom of the neck—that resist ordinary, less dynamic activities.

ACTIVITY	CALORIES BURNED
Using high-quality whip (per gentle stroke) . . . . 12 Handle should be made of fine Italian leather wrapped around ebony with good balance and, to add to the fun, should have a built-in FM radio. (Versace's fall whip line showed promise.)	
If partner pleading, "Harder, harder." 17	
Accommodating partner 500	
Pausing for a Pepsi 3	

WEIGHT LOSS BONUS #12: DOMINATION

ACTIVITY	CARB GRAMS BURNED

Spanking (per spank) 7
The simplest and most stimulating form of
spanking is laying your partner across your
knees, adjusting his gladiator outfit (or, if you
seek historical accuracy, his slave panties), and
gently smacking the buttocks either with the
open hand or his favorite novel. (Avert tragedy
by making certain partner is lying facedown.)
Should your hand grow tired, feel free to use
your partner's. For a significant increase in
calories burned, alter the above procedure by
holding partner across your knees while you
remain standing. For those too exhausted for
manual tasks, but who still wish to enjoy some
form of discipline, we suggest relaxing in bed
and ordering your partner around.

Giving partner orders (per order) 12
The submissive but demanding partner will not
be content with minor commands such as "Kiss
my feet," "Kneel," and "About face." More
effective will be excerpts from your "honey-do"
list:

- "Wash the windows!"
- "Load the dishwasher!"
- "Make that bathroom sparkle!"
- "Empty the dishwasher!"
- "Put up the storm windows!"
- "Vacuum those drapes!"
- And the all-purpose: "You missed a spot!"

Heighten the drama by ending all commands
with "slave," as in "Fetch my slippers, bring
me a glass of white wine, and then unclog the
sink, slave."

SEX WITH WILDLIFE

Those who can't take criticism or have difficulty with human contact occasionally turn to the animal kingdom in their time of need, since the risk of being criticized or having to buy him or her a gift is virtually nil.* The drawbacks are a lack of meaningful communication and, with lions, being eaten. Additionally, noted sex therapist Gretchen Cormorant maintains, in her book *Twilight at the Zoo*, that having unprotected sex with an animal can produce severe psychological consequences, especially for the animal—unless, after lovemaking, you cuddle.

ACTIVITY	CALORIES BURNED
A love-starved burro	20
A Swedish gazelle	77

*You may have to buy them dinner, but that's pretty much it.

A sheep:	
Regular	22
Blow-up	8
An emotionally unavailable owl	15
A demure duck	9
A hunter's decoy	1
An elk:	
Au naturel	80
Wearing a French maid's outfit	111
A frog with a ponytail	16

THING OFTEN SAID AFTER SEX WITH AN ANIMAL

ACTIVITY	CALORIES BURNED
"Will I see you again?"	18

GROUP SEX

ACTIVITY	CALORIES BURNED

Introducing yourself:

    Verbally 6

    Handing out your business card 9

    Just pointing to your name tag 2

Overcoming inhibitions:

    The first time 124

    Your hundredth time 3

Swapping partners 34

If other person gets the better deal 70

Jealousy (partner having more
fun than you) 19

Guilt (you're having more fun
than partner) 55

Anger 18
(You realize that you're wanted for your body
and not your mind, especially difficult to cope
with if you're the attorney general.)

Finding your clothes 5

In the dark 20

KEEPING
A JOURNAL

In addition to this book, maintaining your own record of sexual activity will be helpful for achieving your weight loss goals. You needn't go into detail; just list the activities and calories consumed. Here's a typical entry in the soon-to-be-published journal of one of our women dieters about a pleasant, low-key sexual experience that soon blossomed into love.

JUNE 15: SEX WITH MIKE

ACTIVITY	CALORIES BURNED
Explaining how	12
Suggesting we try something really different	4
Calming a frightened Mike	22
Suggesting things might go better if he took off the massive gold chain around his neck (met in a jewelry chat room)	18
Foreplay (a little of this, a little of that)	36

ACTIVITY	CALORIES BURNED

Intercourse:

Missionary (regular: me on top,
Mike on bottom) 45

Double Helix (both on top) 155

Simultaneous orgasm (photo finish) 100

Thanking Mike for not mussing my hair 8

Asking him to sign my guest book 7

Asking him to take the garbage on
the way out 10

Blowing him a kiss 2

Total time: 64 minutes (limo waiting)
Total calories: 419

PERSONAL WORKSHEET

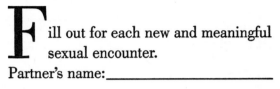

Fill out for each new and meaningful sexual encounter.

Partner's name:_____

Partner's phone number
(for Google search): _____

Social Security number (for
advanced Google search):_____

Where met (singles bar, online ad,
bookstore, fix-up by spinster aunt,
stoplight): _____

Physical appearance (check one):

□ Hunk

□ Hunkette

□ Cute

□ Gorgeous

□ Can't believe my luck

Major asset:_____

_____

Major drawback (may need several
encounters to find this out): _____

Time spent in bed: _____

Time spent making love (if same as
above, write "same"):_____

What was the best part?_____

What was the terrific part? _____

Postlovemaking refreshments: _____

_____

Would you see this person again?
□ Absolutely.
□ Would I? In a New York minute.
□ Not sure.
□ Only if I'm asked.

Estimated calories burned: _____

SEX IN THE CITY

ACTIVITY	CALORIES BURNED
Shades up	355
Shades down	122

8 COMMON DURING-SEX DISTRACTIONS ENCOUNTERED BY CITY LOVERS:

1. Sirens.

2. Patter of big feet (the upstairs neighbors).

3. Patter of little feet (mice).

4. Super demanding his Christmas tip.

5. Car alarms.

6. Construction.

7. Civil unrest.

8. Chinese food arriving.

THE SECOND
HONEYMOON

ACTIVITY	CALORIES BURNED
Older man, younger wife:*	
If he married her for love	87
If she married him:	
For money	50
To get out of Omaha	82
Older man, trophy wife	100
Older woman, trophy husband	347
Older woman with:	
Boy toy	178
Action toy	400
(Only 25 calories if batteries not included.)	

*Often because of midlife crisis, or she's his nanny.

SENIOR SEX

Lovers over fifty who decide not to age often turn to sex instead of bee pollen and kelp.* Not only does it give extra meaning to the phrase "Early Bird Special," but, as one fifty-eight-year-old explained, "It keeps my boyfriend's prostate humming right along." (Many seniors, alas, decline sex, believing it will make them look younger than they actually are and force them, when entering a movie theater, to pay full admission.)

VENUE	CALORIES BURNED
A Winnebago† 74	

("Especially kind to our backs," raved one over-sixty-five couple who claim they have had sex, in their RV, in all forty-nine states and most of Manitoba.)

---

*In his landmark study *Guano: Why Bats Fear Their Own Sexuality*, Dr. Babcock Dingly, holder of the Chair That Doesn't Wobble at Golda's Bible College, concluded that couples over sixty who engage in vigorous sex five or more times weekly are the least likely to complain that their children never call.

†It's the partner who had the most fun who apologizes for holding up traffic.

Without tinted windows 158
(There's a 25-calorie bonus if the excitement
makes your "Don't come knockin' if the
trailer's rockin'" bumper sticker fall off.)

A Mercury Grand Marquis 55
(There's a 15-calorie bonus if wild sex makes
your "Wishin' I was fishin'" bumper sticker
peel.)

A gated community:

Luxury development 139

Prison 27

WATCHING "BETTER SEX" MOVIES

Afairly passive activity, but appropriate for lovers intent on exploring their sexuality while eating popcorn.

ACTIVITY	CALORIES BURNED
In a theater	49
Spotted by someone from the office	200
Renting raincoat	10
At your computer:	
Home	23
Office	55
War room	70
Growing aroused	49
Because of what the actors are doing	77
Because you recognize your spouse	233

SENDING YOUR LOVER TO RENT AN ADULT VIDEO — CALORIES BURNED

If she returns with:

Willing Wenches of Marymount	55
Dumpster Chicks in Heat	80
The Matrix	3

LOVERS' QUARRELS

Whether it's a tiff, a spat, a heated discussion, or just a minor disagreement over whether a new ironing board is appropriate for Valentine's Day, loving couples actually look forward to controversy, since, once in bed, the make-up *Oh-my-God-let's-never-argue-again* sex can propel them well into the next century.

ACTIVITY	CALORIES BURNED
Arguing over:	
Who's more wonderful	11
Who's better in bed	13
Who loves whom more	15
A suspicious motel charge	233
Where to spend Thanksgiving	37

ACTIVITY	CALORIES BURNED

Arguing over sex:

Where to have it 20

When to have it 25

Whether to have it 51

Whose turn it is to feed the baby 14

Whether to bother feeding the baby 40

Prayer in school 24

Prayer in the bedroom 80

JEALOUSY: PART I

A normal human emotion, usually aroused when one lover discovers trace elements, real or imagined, of a rival. The result can be anything from a vague mental discomfort to the inability to keep solids down.

Jealousy aroused by partner's:

Sudden increase in business dinners 45

Sudden interest in losing weight
and working out 49

Being extra-considerate to you 51

Change of cologne 66

Change of wardrobe 76

Taking hushed calls in the next room 41

And not inviting you to say hello 99

Unexplained absences (two or
more weeks) 118

Unexplained past 300

Observing partner leaving motel
at 3:30 P.M. 20

And you're pretty sure he's
not the desk clerk 148

Catching partner in bed with someone 160

The neighbor's dog 528

JEALOUSY: PART II

If you know your lover's password, give yourself 100 calories for each incriminating e-mail you discover.

ACTIVITY	CALORIES BURNED
Going through lover's drawers	34
While he's wearing them	258
Finding:	
Love letters	3
Not yours	519
Matchbook from Hooter's	122
Receipt for bracelet that, after you checked, is definitely not on *your* wrist	177
Obsessive behavior:	
Sniffing lover the moment he gets home	13
Lover asking, "Do you smell something burning?"	5
Responding, "Yes, me."	37

Dusting lover for fingerprints 53
(Easier to do when lover sleeping.)
500-calorie bonus if you spot your lover,
who's supposed to be out of town, pushing a
baby carriage while walking happily arm-in-
arm with a beaming companion.

SEX IN THE WORKPLACE

Who has time?" groaned a supervisor at our Know Your Erogenous Zones corporate seminar. To those who think mixing business with pleasure is unprofessional, we say nonsense —not only does it improve job performance, it's also a hands-on way to network. There are, however, certain conventions you need to observe:

1. If it's dress-down Friday, don't wear a bustier.

2. Urging, "Faster, I have a golf date" will make the most devoted partner feel used.

3. If you're tactful, it's not inappropriate to ask for a raise while coupling with a superior (unless it's during the Christmas party).

4. When at your workstation, it's permissible to have sex in the carpal tunnel position.

5. If it's an "office visit," have your assistant hold all calls and light candles. It shows you're romantic.

6. According to federal OSHA guidelines, a superior is obligated to make sure the underling climaxes first.

7. Sweet nothings often uttered during sex in the workplace:
   • "Tell him I'll call him back."
   • "So, how'd you like my résumé?"
   • "I'm getting closer—hand me your mouse."

8. After-five trysts entitle you to supper money—lots of it.

9. Should you hate yourself for doing it?

NO IF:	YES IF:
It gets you out of the mail room.	It turns out to be the wrong career move.

10. Sex in the workplace: Advantage: You're on company time. Disadvantage: You're on company furniture.

THE NOONER

Something to consider if you just met someone special, perhaps a coworker, but are not yet certain whether they're worth an entire evening.

ACTIVITY	CALORIES BURNED
Parking vehicle where it can't be seen from the road:	
Sporty little Saab convertible	4
Tractor trailer	109
Checking into motel	8
Demanding corporate rate	25
Undressing	25
If motel charges by the hour	300
Talking business in bed:	
Because it gets you excited	11
So you can write off the motel room	45
Safe sex (swearing each other to secrecy)	30
Safer sex (making certain no one sees you leaving)	74

ADVANTAGES OF DAYTIME LOVEMAKING

1. Easier to get a motel room.

2. You can also watch soaps.

3. All stores are open. If sex was disappointing, you can still go shopping.

APPEARING IN PUBLIC UNDER THE INFLUENCE OF LUST: HOW TO LOOK LIKE YOU'RE NOT HAVING TONS OF STEAMY SEX

If you live in a conservative community, it doesn't behoove you to appear in public—say, at a prayer breakfast—with a hickey the size of Tulsa. We try, for the sake of (a) our image and (b) the nation, to never appear wanton or, in the words of one of our earthier panel members, "Like we get it regular." If, however, you're one of those unfortunate individuals who can't help but exude sexual charisma, even when wearing Birkenstocks, the following sartorial advice may help you at least tone it down.

1. According to our Lust Task Force, the best way to conceal a smoldering sexuality is the golf outfit, preferably one comprising a floppy straw sun hat, vivid lime shirt, and white pants (possibly embroidered with little fish) with a white belt. (Note re: pants: Be sure the seat hangs down. This discourages ogling and conceals the fact that you have a buff and curvaceous butt.)

2. A shawl, preferably one crocheted by a kindly grandmother, furthers the "I hardly ever think about sex" image. It should be wrapped protectively around the shoulders, as though you were standing on the deck of an ice cutter patrolling the Bering Sea (doubly effective if shawl-wearer a male).

3. Wear your pants pulled up high, for best results just below your chest. This accentuates that much-sought-after "Sex? What's that?" pear-shaped look.

4. Whenever possible, women with terrific legs should wear flats that (a) de-eroticize those glorious calves, (b) neutralize the ankles, and (c) make their feet look bigger and flatter—so they resemble two flounders.

5. Underwear. For men, baggy boxers or a Speedo with cuffs. Prim women should shun decadent products from Victoria's Secret and Frederick's of Hollywood, instead relying on flannel dainties from either L.L. Bean or the gift boutique of the National Rifle Association.

6. Men blessed with white, skinny legs might consider a yellow terry cabana set with sandals and socks. Makes a proud "I haven't had it in years" statement when worn in strong sunlight or an American Legion lodge.

7. Sun-damaged skin, the result of hours of lawn croquet, gardening, and yachting, is a plus.

XI.
MISCELLANEOUS
PROBLEMS,
EMERGENCIES,
AND DISASTERS

*Most serious accidents occur within fifty miles
of one's bed.**

—NOVA PILBEAM, LLOYD'S OF HACKENSACK

In the following pages, we list the calories burned while coping with stress situations, ranging from shock at seeing a rail-thin supermodel naked to annoyance at a partner who, on climaxing, asks you to buy land in the Poconos. All are easily survivable if you have a sense of humor, or can get dressed quickly.

*There are exceptions. An Iraqi exchange student fell off his moped while touring Versailles, and an overweight American collapsed on a beach chair while sunning himself in Cannes.

PENIS ENVY

ACTIVITY	CALORIES BURNED
For woman	3
For man	72
For a bisexual pipefitter named Maurice	90
For new transsexual:	
Eloise to Anthony	144
Anthony to Eloise	3
Clyde to Humphrey	240

TYPICAL SEX-RELATED FEARS

ACTIVITY	**CALORIES BURNED**
Partner hates me for what I did	8
Partner hates me for what I didn't do	17
At any moment our weekend guest will enter the room and quietly sit down	10
Does partner think I'm too fat?	20
Climaxed too soon (just as partner was getting ready)	9
Climaxed too late (just as partner was leaving)	16
Didn't climax—can she tell?	28
Partner thinks of me as a sex object	9
Partner doesn't think of me as a sex object	12
Partner won't administer last rites should I not recover from orgasm	80

GUILT: PART II

Frequently used by extreme masochists to compensate when they experience sexual euphoria.

ACTIVITY	CALORIES BURNED
Self-abuse:	
Enjoying it	21
Not enjoying it	3
Liking sex	10
Loving sex	33
Never wanting to stop even if your partner leaves	58
Possible guilt situations:	
1. Despite little formal training, orgasm comes easily, naturally, and spontaneously	49
2. You totally enjoy sex, even though many people in the United States earn less than the minimum wage	15
3. After six hours of sex, your mind begins to wander	8

AGGRAVATION

A lthough science has yet to determine precisely why aggravation burns calories, we do know that people, when aggravated, lose weight, possibly because they stamp their feet or, in extreme cases of aggravation, emit steam. Below are several typical situations encountered during sex.

ACTIVITY	CALORIES BURNED
Partner keeps chattering on about her day	11
Partner insists on including cat in pre-cuddling foreplay	17
Partner just went to the bathroom for the seventh time	22
Smoking a joint	55
During sex, partner is taking phone calls	7
During sex, partner is making phone calls (Permitted if partner a Hollywood agent.)	40
During extra-passionate moments partner asks, "How come we never go anywhere?"	19

Partner comes to bed with eight pounds
of cold cream on her face 65

And wants to do it 100

Rejection 35

It is a sign of rejection if partner:

- Has her sixteenth headache this week.

- Tells you, "I think you're very special."

- Replies, "Whose?" when you ask how she feels about children.

- Keeps a bear trap on her side of the bed.

- Thanks you for your invitation but informs you that she always spends New Year's Eve with her godmother.

- Presents you with a goodnight kiss through a surgical mask.

- Serves you warm aquavit.

- Hasn't made actual eye contact with you for six months.

- Tells you her best sex ever was her body search by security personnel at O'Hare.

- Asks for her books, CDs, and keys to her place back.

- Ends sex with a handshake.

WEIGHT LOSS BONUS #13: GETTING CAUGHT*

etting caught with a partner other than your own can instantly reduce your waistline by one full inch! Calorie counts here are flexible, depending on how open-minded your own partner is or how quickly you can leap through an unopened window.

ACTIVITY	CARB GRAMS BURNED
Denying everything	39
Despite the photos	200

Add 10 calories for each of the following activities:

- Leaping out of bed.
- Attempting to remain calm.
- Trying to explain.
- Stuttering.
- Insisting you weren't having that much fun.
- Running with just one shoe on.

*Relationship experts tell us that it's far easier to have an extra-marital affair if you're single.

FIGHTING
OFF PETS

Take comfort: Having sex under adverse conditions involving animals burns extra calories and makes you appreciate more those private and perfect moments with a wonderful partner.

ACTIVITY	CALORIES BURNED
Tiny nervous dog with annoying bark	3
Playful Saint Bernard	44
Jealous Doberman	50
Possessive pit bull	97
Enraged Akita	50
The neighbor's cat	10
Resentful budgie	3½
Determined mosquito	33

WHEN THE UNTHINKABLE HAPPENS

Various crises during sex, other than hecklers, may threaten the magic mood. The remedies are (a) to have an understanding partner and (b) to keep going no matter what.

ACTIVITY	CALORIES BURNED
Cramp:	
Leg	11
Menstrual	45
Chafed elbows	19
(Caused by making love on bargain sheets with a negative thread count.)	
Bedsores (see above)	27
Acid flashback	38
Acid reflux	72
Chest pains from:	
Your heart	44
His medals	90
Her implants	190

ACTIVITY	CALORIES BURNED

Menopause:

   For her 22

   For him 75
   (If he's the one experiencing hot flashes,
   90 calories.)

Rope burns 30

Floss burns 4
(Sex between dentists.)

WHEN SEX TAPERS OFF

ACTIVITY	CALORIES BURNED
Memories	32
Assisted by video from camera hidden above bed	170

Eleven uses for an ex-lover should things not work out:

1. Good friend
2. Furniture mover
3. Palimony
4. Recipe tester
5. Compost
6. Character witness
7. Organ donor
8. Source of new dates
9. Dog walker
10. Sex (strictly platonic)
11. Sex (strictly practice)

XII.
PROCREATION

Dieting couples trying to start a family will find the weight loss benefits immense, particularly if the male partner has an iffy sperm count and asks, after every orgasm, "Do you think you got pregnant this time?" Additionally, since you're having sex for procreation rather than pleasure, suppressing the side effects of pleasure —moaning, ecstasy, and feeling sticky— will burn extra calories (not to mention carb grams).

Also contributing to weight loss are related activities such as:

ACTIVITY	CALORIES BURNED
Staring longingly at couples pushing a carriage	23

Worrying over whether you can
really afford to start a family 150
(But only 2 carb grams if eager future
grandparents have already started a college
trust fund.)

Wondering if the baby photos
will come out 3½

*Note: Once pregnancy occurs, and to minimize
weight gain, sex should continue so long as
you (a) heed the advice of your physician and
(b) can find a comfortable position.*

16 REASONS TO START A FAMILY

1. Your in-laws own a toy store.

2. You both want children.

3. With your genes, intelligence, and looks, you owe it to the world.

4. Maybe it'll improve your marriage?

5. Your biological clock is ticking and he hears it.

6. Birth control pills = bloat.

7. You will kill them if you hear your parents or in-laws say, "So when are you giving us grandchildren?" one more time.

8. Need someone to carry on the family name.

9. Need another tax deduction.

10. Just used the last condom and too lazy to go out for more.

11, House too neat.

12. That spare bedroom looks so lonely.

13. The cats just aren't doing it for you any longer.

14. Prefer the patter of little feet to be a child rather than mice.

15. Can't depend on migrant labor.

16. For Hannukah, in-laws gifted you a donor egg.

TRYING TO CONCEIVE

ACTIVITY	CALORIES BURNED
Simplified version:	
Observing glint in partner's eye	6
Undressing	17
Sex	85
Luck (pregnant on first try!)	22
Complicated version:	
Calculating optimal times using:	
Calendar	14
Tea leaves	88
Writing checks to fertility centers	131
Trying to get a refund	500
Trying and trying:	
For her	27
For him	288
For mattress	50
In vino veritas	10
In vitro veritas	80

PREGNANCY TEST: POSITIVE!

A nnouncing to your family and coworkers that you're pregnant burns a mere 10 calories. It's that special, intimate moment when you tell the father-to-be that consumes the calories.

ACTIVITY	CALORIES BURNED
Telling him the good news	33
If he replies:	
"Wow, darling, that's wonderful."	30
"Can't this wait until halftime?"	45
"Is it mine?"	90
"Is it yours?"	200
Celebrating	77
Dancing around room with spouse	141
With anonymous donor	300
With test tube	3
Ignoring government warning (just this once)	60
(Sharing bottle of Dom Perignon.)	

ACTIVITY	CALORIES BURNED

Telling boss the good news:

If company has liberal maternity leave policy 12	
If not 55	

WEIGHT LOSS BONUS #14: APPETITE

ACTIVITY	CARB GRAMS BURNED
Morning sickness 24	
(Includes nausea, running to bathroom, getting sick, all that fun stuff.)	
Evening appetite 0	

MIDNIGHT CRAVINGS (HERS)

CRAVING	CALORIES GAINED
Gingerbread muffin	356
Blueberry cheesecake (entire)	2,488
Cheeseburger	467
French fries (45)	510
1 leek	½
1 pint Häagen-Dazs Chocolate Chocolate	1,100
Pastrami on white toast	566
Fried squid dipping sauce	85
2 Chiclets	10
Cheese-stuffed ravioli (25)	317
Fried chicken (entire)	1,593
Hot dog	196

*Point of Etiquette for Fathers-to-Be: To
instantly satisfy his wife's desires, the
considerate husband keeps a hot plate, a little
refrigerator, and a fork on his side of the bed.*

SEX SUBSTITUTES

Because it's often difficult to feel sexy with (a) a backache, (b) nausea, (c) gas, or (d) elastic pants, we offer the following nearly-as-good alternatives.

ACTIVITY	CALORIES BURNED
Counting loot from the baby shower	31
Doctor's check-ups	77
Painting baby's room:	
You	732
Supervising your husband	88
Wondering if you'll ever again:	
Regain your figure	12
Fit into that slinky black cocktail dress	40
Watching your breasts enlarge	47
Watching your husband watch your breasts enlarge	70

GIVING BIRTH

ACTIVITY	CALORIES BURNED
Contractions:	
For her (per contraction) 2	
For him (per contraction):	
If he's calm 3	
If he panics 40	
Labor (regular) 1,300	
Triplets 3,900	
With husband assisting:	
Offering encouragement .... 22 (Wiping wife's head, yelling either "Push!" or "I need a drink.")	
Holding camera steady 60	
Fainting 4	
Thanking obstetrician 20	
Thanking stork 8	

WAITING TO RESUME SEX

ACTIVITY	CALORIES BURNED
Until you get home from the hospital	266
Until you pay off the hospital bill	2,645
Until you decide whom baby most resembles	123
Until baby's first:	
Smile	90
Tooth	245
Until you're ready for the next baby	114
Until baby goes off to college	17,500

Point of Marital Etiquette: Who gets up in the middle of the night to feed baby? If baby is nursing, the wife (or a husband with an absurdly high estrogen count). Etiquette dictates, however, that the husband remain fully awake in sympathy until she returns to bed.

THE HEIGHT REPORT (SIZE MAY COUNT)

Lovers who work out should take into account muscle mass, bone density, and the skin fold test (fold skin in half; if it creases, you're in good shape).

IF YOU ARE	YOU SHOULD BE		
	Small frame	Medium frame	Large frame
14 to 30 lbs.	2 ft. 1 in.	2 ft. 3 in.	2 ft. 5 in.
31 to 42 lbs.	2 ft. 4 in.	2 ft. 7 in.	3 ft.
43 to 54 lbs.	2 ft. 9 in.	3 ft.	3 ft. 3 in.
55 to 65 lbs.	3 ft. 2 in.	3 ft. 7 in.	4 ft. ½ in.
66 to 77 lbs.	3 ft. 9 in.	4 ft. 1 in.	4 ft. 4 in.
78 to 90 lbs.	4 ft.	4 ft. 4 in.	4 ft. 7 in.
91 to 100 lbs.	4 ft. 5 in.	4 ft. 9 in.	5 ft.
101 to 110 lbs.	4 ft. 10 in.	5 ft. 1 in.	5 ft. 3 in.
111 to 122 lbs.	5 ft.	5 ft. 2 in.	5 ft. 5 in.
123 to 135 lbs.	5 ft. 3 in.	5 ft. 5 in.	5 ft. 7 in.

IF YOU ARE	YOU SHOULD BE		
	Small frame	Medium frame	Large frame
136 to 147 lbs.	5 ft. 3½ in.	5 ft. 6 in.	5 ft. 9 in.
148 to 160 lbs.	5 ft. 7 in.	5 ft. 9 in.	5 ft. 11 in.
161 to 172 lbs.	5 ft. 8 in.	5 ft. 10 in.	6 ft. ½ in.
173 to 185 lbs.	5 ft. 9 in.	6 ft.	6 ft. 2 in.
186 to 200 lbs.	5 ft. 10 in.	6 ft. 1 in.	6 ft. 4 in.
201 to 212 lbs.	5 ft. 11 in.	6 ft. 2 in.	6 ft. 5 in.
213 to 225 lbs.	6 ft.	6 ft. 3 in.	6 ft. 7 in.
226 to 240 lbs.	6 ft. 4 in.	6 ft. 6 in.	6 ft. 10 in.
241 to 255 lbs.	6 ft. 7 in.	6 ft. 10 in.	7 ft. 2 in.
256 to 270 lbs.	7 ft. ½ in.	7 ft. 3 in.	7 ft. 7 in.
271 to 285 lbs.	7 ft. 3 in.	7 ft. 7 in.	8 ft.

APPENDIX

THE DIETING LOVER'S LOVE SIGNS

The connections between astrology, weight loss, and sex were first noted by the eleventh-century Arab mystic Murray Applebaum, in his now legendary *Hummus Cantata*, a motet for eight voices and blender. A distillation of his wisdom is hereby presented for the following thirteen astrological signs.

AQUARIUS: JANUARY 21–FEBRUARY 19

Your utter aliveness and zest for life have turned you into a sexual over-achiever. You smother your partner with pleasure, and your partner, if he or she is still breathing, reciprocates. You are known for your "kookier than thou" reputation and have the sex toys from a plumbing supply house to prove it. With the right person, you'd gladly settle down in a little white cottage with a picket fence—preferably a 5,000-square-footer with a pool and a butler.

- Outstanding sexual quality: Because you have a high IQ and speak six languages, lovers go to bed with you for your mind. This means you don't have to undress but must hum the third act of *Lohengrin*.

- Sexual turn-ons: Water beds, sex so wild that you can never again look your minister in the eye, and cleaning firearms.

- Sexual turnoffs: Gentle laxatives and firemen in panty hose.

- Most sensitive erogenous zone: You're one big feeling, so you have no nonerogenous zones.

- Secret sexual fantasy: A champagne-and-caviar picnic in a hot-air balloon or, with a lover who's afraid of heights, a Volkswagen.

A hearty sexual appetite keeps you constantly on the lookout for new and profound experiences, especially with lovers with a heat-seeking missile. You are one of the few people able to grasp the connection between inferior sex and juice bars. Your sense of dignity and sheer carnal lust prevent you from sleeping with vegetarians (they rattle), executive chefs named Darius, and anyone enamored of wheatgrass juice.

- Outstanding sexual qualities: Incredible response time when lips are pressed to your thighs plus an uncanny ability to time the stock market.

- Sexual turn-ons: As a lover of humanity, you seek a partner who believes in world peace, saving the environment, and gifts from Neiman Marcus.

- Sexual turnoff: Lack of trust. A new partner, for example, who holds on to her purse during sex and frisks you before you leave.

- Most sensitive erogenous zones: Your inner wrist and the back of your neck.
- Secret sexual fantasies: To have sex during an MRI and to just once make love on a revolving bed without experiencing motion sickness.

ARIES: MARCH 21–APRIL 20

A born ruler, you seek submissive lovers who do eerie things to compensate for their rigid childhood—you have twice had sex with a leprechaun. You are renowned for supplementing the sex act with a catcher's mitt, leather chaps, and a pitcher of daiquiris. You never let yourself get too carried away, however, and have yet to do anything that would disgrace a Hell's Angel.

- Outstanding sexual qualities: Heart of a lover, hands of a surgeon, great malpractice insurance.
- Sexual turn-ons: A lover who leaves wicked messages on your voice mail at work, which you play for your coworkers when you return from lunch drunk.

- Sexual turnoffs: Botched circumcisions and a partner who prefers Internet porn sites to you.
- Most sensitive erogenous zones: Your brain, your lower back, and the third shelf of your refrigerator.
- Secret sexual fantasy: After making torrid love in the crisp, cool air of a mountaintop, seeing your weary partner carried off by a large bird.

TAURUS: APRIL 21–MAY 21

Sizzling, sexual, and endowed with incredible staying power, the torchy Taurus believes that sex is for any time, any place, as long as it doesn't violate community standards. You are constantly alert for amorous indulgence and have had sex everywhere, including on a Ferris wheel at midnight, the outskirts of Sheboygan, and under a boardwalk (during which time you were washed out to sea and never heard from again).

- Outstanding sexual qualities: You're a cheap date—you get crazy on just one glass of wine, a morsel of seared tuna, and a free tote bag.

- Sexual turn-ons: Clean socks, long moonlight walks in the rain with a partner who has an umbrella, and a musical bedpan that, when sat upon, plays "Hail to the Chief."

- Sexual turnoffs: Rodents, and lovers who fidget and try to change the subject when you ask about (a) their past and (b) your future.

- Most sensitive erogenous zones: Eyelids, under the jaw, and any humidor filled with illegal Cuban cigars.

- Secret sexual fantasy: A long and relaxing shiatsu massage by the technique's inventor, Nigel Shiatsu.

GEMINI: MAY 22–JUNE 21

Although dazzlingly attractive and wildly alluring (those bedroom eyes are registered with Interpol), a combination of indifferent parents and attending the wrong prep schools has made you insecure. You find it difficult to express your sexual needs except by e-mail or, if your computer's down, by micromanaging your lover's hand.

- Outstanding sexual qualities: You are a feast for the eyes, cost mere pennies a day to operate, and, if necessary, can moan in Yiddish.

- Sexual turn-ons: Hawaiian swing music, that sugar rush after chugging a pint of maple syrup, and lovers who ask, "How do you stay so thin?"

- Sexual turnoffs: Right-wing conspiracies and lovers who, immediately after a huge climax, cease to have a detectable pulse.

- Most sensitive erogenous zones: Above the waist, below the waist, and the equator.

- Secret sexual fantasy: To be invited, on opening day of baseball season, to throw out the first fan.

A late bloomer, you've been making up for lost time—you've thus far lost two pounds, one of which you shed this past weekend with an alcoholic opera singer named Rex. Unfortunately, you are getting too buff and will have to choose between fewer sexual encounters or increasing your food intake. Smart Cancers do so by sipping hot chocolate instead of Perrier.

- Outstanding sexual qualities: Your swanlike neck has been classified as the fourteenth wonder of the modern world.

- Sexual turn-on: To be wanted, just for once, only for your body, swept off your feet, and taken by limo to the nearest Ramada Inn.

- Sexual turnoffs: Doing your own laundry, Glade, and yeast infections.

- Most sensitive erogenous zones: Shoulders, backs of the knees, and the wishbone.

- Secret sexual fantasy: Hearing your lover's cell phone play "Here Comes the Bride" after you've had great sex.

Your generous and trusting nature and radiant sexuality have gotten you into trouble more than once—after incredible sex, your last lover's first words were, "Could you possibly cash a check?" Danger and adventure, however, continue to be a vital part of your life—you even accept blind dates arranged by your mother. As a lover, you are a superstar; before sex you seldom bother with petty chores like cuddling and letting your nails dry.

- Outstanding sexual qualities: Ten toes and two arches that would satisfy the most demanding foot fetishist, plus four gloriously dimpled cheeks.

- Sexual turn-ons: Origami roses, dart fights, partners named Bubba, and belt buckles proclaiming, "Free mustache rides."

- Sexual turnoffs: Sandals worn with socks, cheeseburgers served on matzos, and nude stevedores.

- Most sensitive erogenous zones: Abs, pecs, and any after-hours club with a hot band.
- Secret sexual fantasy: To spend a year in bed with the perfect lover—eating your way through *Larousse Gastronomique*.

VIRGO: AUGUST 24–SEPTEMBER 23

Proud Virgo, you feel that few people meet or even approach your standards—you refuse to have sex just for pleasure, so your lover must also buy you a drink. A noble attitude, but more often than not you find yourself alone on Saturday night, playing video games, wondering about the half-life of those empty pizza boxes, and eating cheap store-brand ice cream with your fingers. Your unwillingness to compromise, however, pays off. When you meet the right one, there's no holding back. You shower your partner with love, sex, and crumbs from the Krispy Kremes that give you ample energy to experience multiple orgasms and then get up early Sunday morning for Mass.

- Outstanding sexual qualities: Total belief in the Golden Sexual Rule: Do unto my partner as I would have my partner do unto me (unless I'm paying for it).

- Sexual turn-ons: The new intern's buns and spending three hours in bed with your lover after a really intense phone fight.

- Sexual turnoffs: Another hike in postage rates, and a full body cavity search by a stranger wearing press-on nails.

- Most sensitive erogenous zones: You're not fussy, but the lover who rubs your feet with warm béarnaise sauce instantly gets keys to your place.

- Secret sexual fantasy: To be tied to a giant redwood tree while being licked all over by Adolph.

LIBRA: SEPTEMBER 24–OCTOBER 23

A craving for romance and affection is often frustrated by a practical, no-nonsense side—you put your career first. Even during sex in a dimly lit bedroom you wear your pager, often removing it and striking a match to see who's calling. You find it odd that lovers seldom give you a second chance, but take comfort in the fact that you get at least three calls a week from headhunters (two in Manhattan, one in Borneo). Never mind, though—an understanding partner will soon come along who isn't threatened by your six-figure income and insistence on a background check.

- Outstanding sexual qualities: During sex, you can utter, "Do me, baby, oh do me," without feeling that you've compromised your integrity.

- Sexual turn-ons: A good cry, the miracle of compound interest, and petite partners— they eat less.

- Sexual turnoffs: Day-old mutton, athlete's foot, and Madonna singing Schubert.

- Most sensitive erogenous zones: Backs of thighs, the philtrum, and your safety deposit box.

- Secret sexual fantasies: To open a liquor store in Iraq, and to earn extra bonus miles by being with a lover who lets you do all the work.

Moist sex is your forte. When aroused, you become uncontrollable and have been known to cause flood damage in low-lying areas. This makes you popular with the sensual crowd but not with insurance companies. Your creative gifts and willingness to experiment allow you endless variations on the art of lovemaking—one variation, involving golf shoes and a sarong, has led many partners to believe you need therapy. Wise Scorpio knows better.

- Outstanding sexual qualities: Can't cook, and a complexion that passes muster in even the cruelest light.

- Sexual turn-on: Undressing each other slowly and sensuously while comparing designer labels.

- Sexual turnoffs: Dweebs, Chihuahuas on speed, and partners who go ballistic when you eat tripe in bed.

- Most sensitive erogenous zones: Between the shoulder blades, your eyelids, and Cancún.

- Secret sexual fantasy: A really juicy scandal: Your name is found in a "little black book" owned by a prominent madam. Beside your name is an asterisk indicating "Excellent tipper."

SAGITTARIUS: NOVEMBER 23–DECEMBER 21

Sensual Sagittarius! Just the thought of romance causes heat rash. The time doesn't pass quickly enough until your next tryst. A slave to passion, you are completely vulnerable, finding it nearly impossible to resist a spontaneous sexual encounter, even if the elevator's crowded. The envy of your friends, you hold something of a record: Having been seduced twenty-six times in one day, you still managed to respond to all of your e-mails. You are not promiscuous, however, just hedonistic. When you die, you're going to hell.

- Outstanding sexual qualities: You know the difference between an unwelcome sexual advance and a very welcome sexual advance.

- Sexual turn-ons: Nude beaches with a weight restriction, a cozy New England inn, cuddly toys, and lovers not too proud to beg.

- Sexual turnoffs: Anatomically correct hand puppets, and whistles from construction workers who can't carry a tune.

- Most sensitive erogenous zones: Your thighs and most upscale shoe stores.

- Secret sexual fantasy: During a steamy climax, your partner holds you close and whispers, "Can the liberals take foreign policy back from the Republicans?"

CAPRICORN: DECEMBER 22–JANUARY 20

Despite a somewhat shy and retiring personality, your incredible, unspeakably smoldering lust and abilities in the kitchen keep your phone ringing constantly—you've gotten calls from as far away as Tibet and as near as the coworker on your right. Since discovering sex, you've never had a weight problem and must, in fact, eat several meals a day to keep from becoming transparent. Your rivals secretly envy you but never show it, hoping that someday you'll reveal the secret of your "Enchanted Goulash." Capricorn knows that day will never come.

- Outstanding sexual qualities: Exquisitely sensitive, and can smoke a cigarette like Bette Davis. You love it when attractive strangers brush against you and leer when you take public transportation—as long as they don't pick your pocket.

- Sexual turn-on: A fingertip massage up and down the small of your back (it releases the tension caused by a surprise visit from a Mary Kay rep).

- Sexual turnoffs: Missing your freeway exit, and both a penile and a breast implant on the same person.

- Most sensitive erogenous zone: You're a sucker for a lover gently blowing in your ear or, if lover just ate garlic, using a cordless fan.

- Secret sexual fantasy: Making the researcher blush when he asks about your frequency rate.

A special one-sign-fits-all member of the Zodiac—recommended by maverick astrologers for those either unsure of their birth date or unconvinced that their cusp is correct. To compensate for a feeling of uncertainty, Neons are usually world-class lovers, able to keep up with and often surpass even the most consummate Capricorns. Unless caught stealing towels, Neons are always invited back for more and more, and more. Neons are known for the original touches they bring to lovemaking, such as love bites, wax buildup, and the tunes they play on the kazoo.

- Outstanding sexual qualities: A smooth talker and easily able to have sex in all of the positions suggested by the chickens on the Food Network.

- Sexual turn-ons: Poetry, bailiffs named Zorro, and nude jury duty.

- Sexual turnoffs: The hidden calories in yams, drug tests, and partners who make you lose weight in all the wrong places: sleazy motels, the bed of a pickup truck, or the linen closet.

- Most sensitive erogenous zones: Your lips, your heart, and your wall safe.

- Secret sexual fantasy: To stand up to an arrogant sommelier and send back a bottle of wine, calmly explaining, "It reeks of potatoes."

Richard Smith, the writer-in-residence, has written for several major publications, including *Cosmopolitan*, *The New York Times*, and *Playboy*, and one minor publication (*Pravda*). His books include *The Dieter's Guide to Weight Loss During Sex* (on which he lost eighty-one pounds during his busy season), *The Bronx Diet* (on which he lost ½ pound), *The Newlyweds' Guide to Sex on the First Night* (during which he gained twenty-two pounds), and several *365 Days and Nights of Sex* calendars. He likes hiking, camping, fine dining, concerts, and agriculture.